START MAKING SENSE

START MAKING SENSE

Turning the Lessons of Election 2004 into
Winning Progressive Politics

Edited by

DON HAZEN AND LAKSHMI CHAUDHRY

An AlterNet Book

CHELSEA GREEN PUBLISHING COMPANY
WHITE RIVER JUNCTION, VERMONT

Project Editor: Marcy Brant
Copy Editor: Nancy Ringer
Designer: Peter Holm, Sterling Hill Productions
Design Assistant: Daria Hoak, Sterling Hill Productions

Printed in Canada
First printing, March 2005
10 9 8 7 6 5 4 3 2 1

Library of Congress Cataloging-in-Publication Data
Start making sense : turning the lessons of election 2004 into winning
progressive politics / edited by Don Hazen and Lakshmi Chaudhry.
    p. cm.
"An AlterNet Book."
ISBN 1-931498-84-9 (pbk.)
1. Political participation—United States. 2. Progressivism (United States
politics) 3. United States—Politics and government—2001– I. Hazen, Don.
II. Chaudhry, Lakshmi.
JK1764.S8 2005
324.7'0973—dc22

                                              2005006052

Chelsea Green Publishing Company
Post Office Box 428
White River Junction, VT 05001
(800) 639-4099
www.chelseagreen.com

CONTENTS

LOOKING FORWARD

GETTING ACTIVE

INTRODUCTION

Start *Making Sense* sums up the challenge that progressives, populists, and independents face today. First we have to start making sense of who we are and where we want to go. Then we have to start making sense to the American public so we can get there.

It's time to step up and take charge. Until now, too many of us left politics to the so-called experts. At the expense of our future, we turned a blind eye to how much political consultants, lobbyists, and party insiders represent a permanent "Democratic establishment" that controls the political agenda, which is not our own.

At AlterNet (www.alternet.org), we have been reporting on the events, activities, and debates that have occurred among progressives in recent years—from the response to 9/11 to the Iraq war to the 2004 presidential election. And in a way, we have been both activists and journalists, both involved in and documenting the progressive movement and its actions all along. That is one reason we have become one of the most popular Web magazines for political and cultural news.

Now, we have brought together some of our writers, editors, and experts to write a new story about our political future, while confronting what went wrong in the past election. And, perhaps most important, we want to offer you practical advice about what is necessary to build a progressive majority in America today.

How you look at what happened on November 2, 2004, depends on whether you are an optimist or a pessimist. On the positive side, we accomplished much that can help us as we move forward. On the other hand, it was a botched opportunity. Overall, the Democrats weren't tough enough or smart enough, and all of us need to be far better organized if the conservative stranglehold on government is going to be challenged.

So the election offered material for both hope and despair. This book, however, won't be debating whether the glass is half empty or half full. We've opted instead for realism. The bottom line is that there is too much at stake. With lessons learned, we must go forward.

Start Making Sense is not designed to provide answers; it's too soon for that. We want to help you start thinking, talking, and acting to build a movement to take back America.

With that in mind, this book is organized into three basic sections. The first, "Looking Back," is an attempt to make sense of the stunning loss on November 2, 2004. Among the lessons of the presidential election of 2004 is that Democratic and liberal politics have become far too "top down." From John Kerry and the Democratic National Committee to America Coming Together to national interest organizations, we often end up with one-way communication from the leaders to the members.

Progressives gave hundreds of millions of dollars to Democratic campaigns, and what do we have to show for it? Not much. We still don't have the progressive infrastructure we need for political success. Many strong local groups are still underfunded and understaffed. This top-down approach has to change. Far too much of our money went into the coffers of the media conglomerates for advertising, and lots more of our money bankrolled the salaries of consultants and pollsters. According to the Alliance for Better Campaigns, an astonishing $1.6 billion was spent on television advertising in the election. Overall, more than $2.2 billion was spent in the election.

Many of us share a deep frustration with voter suppression in the
election process itself. We probably will never know for sure what
the real vote count was. But thanks to the perseverance of many
in Ohio and in other states, layers of the electoral onion have
been peeled away, exposing a rotten core. Reforming the system
has to be a big priority.

Also in the first section, we take a close, hard look at what we
are up against. The success of conservatives is based on a powerful
grassroots network that includes churches, American Legion
Halls, gun clubs, small businesses, and so on. To help us make
sense of the recent past, we have picked the brains of some trail-
blazers who are challenging the conventional progressive wisdom:
people like Howard Dean, Arianna Huffington, Adam Werbach,
George Lakoff, and Robert Greenwald.

"Looking Forward," the second section, details the big issues we
need to address and grapple with: the Iraq war, the culture war,
and the economy. In this, we have looked for some fresh ideas and
perspectives from the likes of Naomi Klein, Andy Stern, Thomas
Frank, and Tom Hayden.

The last section, "Getting Active," offers a big-picture perspective—from people like Wes Boyd and Colin Greer—as well as concrete suggestions for what we can all do in our local communities.

It is important to remember that building a democratic movement
is a long-term project. As you'll read in this book, conservatives have
been organizing systematically for thirty-plus years, with steadily
increasing power and effectiveness. Many of us jumped into electoral
politics for the first time during the 2004 campaign, and November
2 was an eye-opener: the system sure needs a whole lot of fixing. But
we can't sit back and wait for 2008. Politics isn't something we can
do every four years, or we'll keep losing—and we'll have lousy candidates to boot.

Now is the time to assert some people power. We need to get
involved in our towns, cities, regions, and states and move away
from focusing only on the national stage. If nothing else, the 2004
election proved once again that all politics is local.

Oh, and one more thing: this book is a living document. Limitations of time and space kept us from including a lot more content. We'll post more articles and general food for thought at www.StartMakingSense.org. We hope that what you read—in this book and on our site—inspires you to get involved and help move progressive politics toward a better future.

Remember: you are the movement.

Don Hazen, AlterNet Executive Editor
Lakshmi Chaudhry, AlterNet Senior Editor
San Francisco
February 2005

LOOKING BACK

UNDERSTANDING
THE ELECTION
1

Making Sense of Election 2004 DON HAZEN

Millions of Americans—young and old, liberals, progressives, and independents—dove into electoral politics with unprecedented fervor, many for the first time, in Bush v. Kerry 2004. Defeating George W. Bush became the biggest cause for progressive and independent Americans since the 1960s. Most of us considered it the most important election of our lifetime. Hundreds of thousands of volunteers spent time in swing states and joined phone banks to persuade people to support Kerry.

A surge of creativity energized these ingenious efforts, which included hundreds of books, a slew of Web sites, and scores of movies and videos, each highlighting the need for change. Groups like Billionaires for Bush and Axis of Eve got people laughing at the inanities of Bush policies. Major rock stars hit the road for benefit concerts, while celebrities appeared in Florida, Ohio, Pennsylvania, and other key states to rally voters for change.

Hundreds of thousands of small donors made political contributions for the first time. Even the billionaires got into the action. George Soros and Peter Lewis became the targets of harsh conservative criticism after contributing millions between them to get George Bush out of office. All in all, the Democrats and groups that supported them raised more money than ever before.

Bush was, in many minds, the worst sort of president—an arrogant bully with radically conservative policies far out of the mainstream. He tricked the country into war on false pretenses, then paid no heed to growing evidence of its disastrous failures. He derided science, let the deficit balloon in order to give tax cuts to the rich, and turned a blind eye as corporations robbed their shareholders, poisoned their communities, and injured their customers. Fundamentalists waiting for the Rapture hung on his words, which his speechwriters shaped for their ears.

When they added it all up—a weak economy, an increasingly unpopular war, soaring health-care costs, and so on—the majority of Americans felt the country was on the wrong track. How could the country vote to reelect this president?

But it did. Much to the shock and dismay of the millions who invested their money, time, energy, and passion to stop George W. Bush and the conservative juggernaut he spearheaded, he received several million more votes than John Kerry. His campaign emerged victorious in the two most hotly contested states, Ohio and Florida, while wresting Iowa and New Mexico away from the Democrats. Of the states that voted "red" in 2000, Bush lost only tiny New Hampshire, a state he had previously taken by just a small margin.

We will be grappling with the emotional and political ramifications of Election 2004 for a long time. The competing analyses of why John Kerry lost the November 2 election reflect an array of thoughtful perspectives, as well as a fair amount of jockeying for position and avoiding responsibility for the debacle.

In looking back, we have to avoid the "if only" syndrome—if only Kerry were more progressive, if only there weren't touch-screen voting machines, if only we could talk better to religious people—there's a long list of "if only's," and all of them are important in assessing what went wrong. But in the end, there is no simple, singular "if only." We've had a rude awakening to how much time and hard work it takes to exercise electoral power in a conservative, consumerist, corporate society in which the opposition is built, as Economic Institute founder Jeff Faux explains, "on a long investment in a grassroots infrastructure aimed at convincing voters beyond their base." Conservatives, he continues, "have been at this for a while, and we continue to ignore it at our peril."

If there is one fundamental lesson to be learned from 2004, it is that "a little more and a little better" won't do the trick. The Democrats did far more, far better, in 2004 than in 2000. And it wasn't just their success in raising money or recruiting volunteers. John Kerry got more votes than any Democrat in history, 5 million more than Gore's 2000 tally. It still wasn't enough.

The 2004 election teaches lessons that are painful to accept. The results mean that our country is in many ways different from what we had thought and wished. More important, they demonstrate that if we want to change the nation's political direction, we must change our own attitudes and behavior.

The Candidate and the Campaign

It is important to remember that no single factor lost this election for the Democrats—not the candidate's message, the culture/values gap, the limits of the get-out-the-vote strategy, or any other commonly identified culprit. It is impossible to separate these individual aspects from one another. All are interrelated, and each reflected the Democrats' and the Kerry campaign's prevailing attitude and approach. To change or improve one would have required the transformation of the entire project.

The web of difficulties stemmed in large part from the Kerry team's isolation from the field, which led it to misjudge the fear factor and its failure to clearly communicate beliefs and values that would resonate with a broader public. Lobbyists and establishment figures shaped the campaign's message, and focus groups took the place of real communication with people outside the centers of power. The top-down nature of the campaign expressed and continues to reflect a fundamental weakness of the Democratic Party.

As for the candidate himself, many have written about John Kerry's failure to establish a "narrative" or connect with his message. Some, like LA Weekly writer and Sore Winners author John Powers, attribute his defeat directly to this failing:

In a polarized country fraught with fear, the electorate will ultimately vote for something rather than nothing.

Like him or not, President Bush is Something. He offers a starkly mythic vision of life that possesses enormous visceral power:

We know that you are frightened of terrorists—we will kill them.

We know you want money—we will cut taxes.

We know you worry that American life has lost its moral center—we will restore traditional values.

In contrast, John Kerry never got beyond being the candidate of Anybody But Bush. Yes, he won the debates. Yes, he had a health-care plan. And yes, he belatedly talked sense about the administration's incompetence in Iraq. But after nearly two years on the stump, his candidacy was still defined by his opponent. Running a depressingly cautious campaign, he failed to create the counter myth—or enunciate the progressive vision of America—that would let him defeat a president whose record made him ripe for the toppling. Kerry's promises looked like nothing.

Political observers like Jeff Faux argue that progressives and independents have to take responsibility for colluding in the process that brought us both Kerry's candidacy and its incoherent message.

But Faux is savvy enough about the process of picking the candidate to know there's more than a little Monday-morning quarterbacking going on now. "We Democrats chose Kerry with eyes wide open," Faux wrote in *American Prospect* on December 6, 2004. "We thought his lack of clear definition and his split-the-difference moderation would make him more credible with swing voters. He didn't need a clear vision; imagery would be enough. He was a war hero to contrast with the draft-dodging George W. Bush. Kerry's incoherence was ours, reflecting the party's widespread lack of confidence in its own message."

So the Democrats ended up with a candidate who was clearly experienced and intelligent, but also wooden and rich, and lacking the kind of strong grassroots support that the Republicans enjoyed. Clearly, a mistake was repeated. Four years ago, the Democrats had a smart, wealthy, wooden candidate, and he didn't relate well to the rank and file either. Still, many thought both Gore and Kerry should have won, because the Democratic Party's values and positions overall reflect those of a majority of American voters. Gore did take the popular vote before the Supreme Court took Florida away from him; Kerry lost the popular vote.

The 2004 election teaches the hard reality that people often vote for the person they identify with because of their moral values, emotional leanings, or religious affiliation, even if that means going against their economic self-interest or supporting someone they believe is leading the country in the wrong direction. For many of us who focus on reason and facts and who look to our leaders for rational answers, it came as a shock to discover that winning three debates handily doesn't necessarily win the hearts and minds of American voters.

And voters identify with a candidate they believe is clear and resolute. As a CNN exit poll on November 2 revealed, only 7 percent of voters said "intelligence" was the most important quality in a candidate, and 91 percent of them voted for Kerry. On the other hand, 17 percent of voters said the most important quality was a candidate who "takes a clear stand on the issues," and almost 80 percent of them voted for Bush.

It is an axiom of politics that election campaigns are created, even unconsciously, in the candidate's image. Kerry's campaign certainly reflected his persona: aloof, wealthy, brainy, and patrician. The campaign was essentially all white and centered on Boston and Washington. Most of its key decision makers were long-established, wealthy "experts" with long records of arrogance—and campaign defeats—behind them. It was not a campaign, or a team, that spoke to the heart and soul of America.

Outside the campaign, liberals, unions, and progressive funders and strategists created their own organizations, which they hoped would form a strong political base, independent but supportive of the Democratic Party. Political action committees (PACs) like MoveOn and 527 groups (named for the section of the tax code that governs them), particularly America Coming Together (ACT), received vast sums in donations. They provided a much-needed boost to the Democratic effort, according to author and historian Michael Kazin. "In Ohio, which decided the election by fewer than 140,000 votes, the extra-party organizations had to do most of the work themselves," Kazin wrote in the January/February 2005 issue of *Mother Jones* magazine. "Not a single Democrat holds statewide office there: the only Buckeye icon Kerry could bring to his rallies was John Glenn, the elderly space hero who retired from the Senate back in 1998."

These PACs and 527s, along with the Kerry campaign itself, also attracted an immense number of volunteers and activists, some well seasoned, some newly minted. But there were problems, caused primarily by the fact that the Kerry campaign and these groups could not coordinate their efforts under the law. For instance, *Salon* writer Farhad Manjoo introduced readers to Moira DeNike, a San Francisco sociology graduate student, a dancer, and a political novice who founded Dancers for Democracy, which raised enough money to send six activists to Miami a few weeks before the Florida registration deadline. DeNike called the ACT office in Florida and was told the group was working on a voter persuasion effort, not voter registration. She called the Kerry campaign in Florida and was told they too were not focused on voter registration, but other groups were.

"What DeNike discovered was that neither the ACT people nor the Kerry people were mounting a final new-registration push in South Florida because each believed that the other group would be handling it," wrote Manjoo. "That would seem to be a silly mistake—didn't people know their rules?—but this sort of thing seems to have occurred often in the campaign, volunteers say."

The campaign finance laws also kept the 527s from working in suburban, small-town, and rural counties, where the Bush campaign so successfully courted swing voters. As Manjoo explained, "ACT could not call on voters to go out and cast a ballot for a specific candidate. In Democratic strongholds, this limitation worked out okay: The group didn't need to sell voters there on the merits of John Kerry, all it had to do was make sure people got to the polls. But how could ACT have campaigned in areas where the voters' preferences weren't so certain? It wouldn't have worked." As a result, likely Democratic voters were overcanvassed, sometimes to the point of annoyance, while regular voters in uncertain districts heard mainly from the Republicans.

But it wasn't just the campaign finance laws that caused the problems. ACT also fell into the same top-down organizational trap as the Democratic Party. Its plans reflected mainly the ideas of one man, Steve Rosenthal, the former political director of the AFL-CIO. Rosenthal's get-out-the-vote model relied on paid canvassers, often outsiders. Todd Gitlin, writing in *Mother Jones* magazine, said the volunteers stuck to the instructions they were given: "Don't get involved in heavy discussions on the block, just figure out which way people are leaning and move on."

The Republicans, by contrast, kept things personal. They worked with about 85,000 trained and committed local volunteers, every one actively engaging his or her neighbors in support of Bush. As Matt Bai wrote in the *New York Times Magazine*, in winning Ohio, "Bush's operatives did precisely what they told me seven months ago they would do . . . they tapped into a volunteer network using local party organizations, union rolls, gun clubs and churches. They backed it up with a blizzard of targeted appeals," direct mail with a sharp focus on the specific hopes and fears voters had identified.

On Election Day, Rosenthal's model couldn't deliver the bacon. It did bring in more voters than Rosenthal himself had anticipated: 554,000 more Ohioans voted for Kerry than had voted for Gore. But it was a day late and a dollar short. The strategy turned out to be based on the realities of 2000. The realities of 2004 had slipped from view. Matt Bai explained that Republicans had adapted to the new realities of suburban and ring counties in Ohio and were able to "mobilize a stunning turnout" among white, conservative, and religious voters. "This effort wasn't visible to Democrats because it was taking place on an entirely new terrain, in counties that Democrats had some vague notion of, but which they never expected could generate so many votes," Bai wrote. "The 10 Ohio counties with the highest turnout percentages, many of them small and growing, all went for Bush, and none of them had a turnout rate of less than 75 percent."

The Kerry campaign, the 527s, and PACs like MoveOn had performed what seemed a remarkable feat: Kerry's swing-state vote increased 21 percent over Gore's in 2000, and nationwide, Kerry garnered 5 million more votes than Gore did in 2000. Bush, unfortunately, improved his numbers by 9 million over 2000, and his swing-state numbers were up by 23 percent over 2000. The ground had shifted beneath the experts' feet.

Tapping the Grass Roots

The results in Ohio exposed a number of shocking new realities. Most important, they upended assumptions about the Democrats being the party of inclusion and small d democracy. As Kazin noted in his *Mother Jones* article, "Through most of its history, the Democratic Party was the natural home of hard-pressed, unglamorous America—manual workers, dirt farmers, small businessmen just a bad month away from bankruptcy. . . . Most Democratic stalwarts were male, and nearly all were white. But they still proudly considered themselves the bone and sinew of a 'people's party.'"

Somewhere along the line, though, Republicans successfully paired the word *liberal* with *elite* in the minds of many Americans. Meanwhile, the right invested heavily in building the numbers of Republican troops on the ground. As Rob Stein explains, Republicans have trained over 30,000 rank-and-file members at the Leadership Institute during the past three decades. Active and influential members of their communities who are also trained

spokespeople for the Republican message, they form the core of
the conservative base.

On a wider scale, as Barbara Ehrenreich points out, evangelical megachurches are replacing government for millions of people, often, ironically, using federal funding to do it. They offer the solace of faith, the promise of community, the structure of sanctioned beliefs. They also provide their members with food, job training, emergency shelter, and other services that Democrats have traditionally considered the government's work. And they do it all while preaching a relentlessly conservative message.

In direct contrast to these close links between the Republicans and their truest believers, the Democratic Party and its activists have trouble forming a working unit, which contributed to the lack of coherence in Kerry's campaign message. Jeff Faux explains the problem:

"While the grassroots center-left—labor, environmentalists, the activist nongovernmental organizations—are expected to mobilize the voters on Election Day," he wrote, "the message they carry is in the hands of the party's Washington-based centrist managers. Heavily influenced by lobbyists, they try to formulate language that keeps the faithful motivated and at the same time does not alienate their corporate clients. Not surprisingly, the message is compromised and foggy, and neither the party's rank and file nor its leadership is able to articulate very well what the party stands for."

The fact that so many progressives define themselves as outside and decidedly separate from the Democratic Party establishment just adds to this weakness. In addition, a large chunk of the progressive and liberal political establishment works for nonprofits, with two major consequences. First, these people often become advocates for individual issues—the environment, gun control, women's rights, labor rights, you name it. They're not as involved in crafting a political vision that weaves all the strands together. Second, many of them play no active role in electoral politics because they are hamstrung by laws that prevent them from partisan activity or they are funded by risk-adverse foundations, which advise them to limit their involvement in order to protect their institutions' nonprofit status.

Plus, some parts of the Democratic base seem to be shrinking. Between the party's own efforts and those of the independent groups, a great deal of work went into campaign mobilization and the so-called ground game. As far as minority registration and turnout goes, these efforts had some real success, increasing the percentage of minorities as part of the electorate from 19 percent in 2000 to 23 percent in 2004, in itself a very promising advance. Yet they ran into trouble holding some traditionally Democratic groups, notably Hispanics. As Jorge Ramos of Univision News noted, if Kerry had won a total of just 64,000 more Hispanic votes in Colorado, Nevada, and New Mexico, he would have taken the White House. Ramos chided the Kerry campaign for taking Latinos for granted, although Kerry took 65 percent of their vote, according to the William C. Velasquez Institute. Four years earlier, Gore took 62 percent. Kerry's margin over Gore is larger than the percentages make it appear, because 7.6 million Hispanics voted in 2004, an increase of 1.6 million (27 percent) over 2000.

Even more noteworthy and ominous, however, was the 5 percent increase in Bush's already wide margin of victory among white voters, since white voters make up 77 percent of voters overall.

According to Bob Wing, national cochair of United for Peace and Justice and founding editor of *ColorLines* magazine, it wasn't white men, but white women, who gave Bush a significant advantage. Although Bush received a large majority of white male votes, the 62 to 37 percent spread marked just a one-point increase over 2000. Among white *women*, however, the percentage who preferred Bush shot up from one point in 2000 to eleven points, 55 to 44 percent, in 2004. That shift made the difference.

According to political analyst Ruy Teixeira, "The last three elections (2000, 2002, 2004) have all had strong 'culture war' components that have severely depressed white working class support for Democrats. Recall that Bill Clinton actually carried the white working class (whites without a four-year college degree) by a point in both his election bids. But in 2000, Al Gore lost these voters by 17 points." In 2004, exit polls suggest that Democrats lost white voters by five percentage points more than in 2000.

"Democrats cannot win when they do so badly among this very large constituency," wrote Teixeira.

The Democrats' loss of white voters showed itself most acutely outside of cities. The political distance between urban centers and small towns or rural areas clearly shaped the outcome in Ohio. Democrats made significant gains in the areas surrounding Columbus and Cleveland, racking up 52,000 more votes than Gore received in 2000. But the Republicans countered these efforts with a huge increase in rural and exurban areas—where turnout was significantly higher. In the end, after all the effort, the Democrats lost Ohio by 2.5 percent instead of 3.5 percent in 2000.

Matt Bai starkly expressed the implications of this change:

> Democrats operated on the premise that they were superior in numbers, if only because their supporters lived in such concentrated urban communities. If they could mobilize every Democratic vote in America's industrial centers—and in its populist heartland as well—then they would win on math alone. Not anymore. Republicans now have their own concentrated vote, and it will probably continue to swell. Turnout operations like ACT can be remarkably successful at corralling the votes that exist, but turnout alone is no longer enough to win a national election for Democrats. The next Democrat who wins will be the one who changes enough minds.

When we reflect on how to gain political power nationally, all thoughts have to start local. Michael Kazin reminds us that the United States is "a nation whose citizens revere volunteerism and local decision making and mistrust politicians who craft their ads and speeches to fit the latest survey." He makes his own proposal for the future:

A reborn Democratic Party would draw ideas and energy from states and local communities, enlisting candidates and organizers who share the values and language of the people whose votes they'll be seeking. It could sponsor comedy nights and dance parties and debates about whether one can support gay marriage and still be a good Christian; throw street festivals at which every immigrant society, sportsmen's club, church, temple, and mosque feels welcome; offer a place for seniors to meet and for community organizers to gather. In a word, it could act a great deal more like the people's party of old, and less like a traveling circus that folds its tents after the first Tuesday in November.

This is not to suggest that a campaign organization has to be democratic—in a short-term battle, an effective command-and-control hierarchy is clearly necessary. The haphazard coordination within and among the various organizations supporting Kerry, even if unavoidable under current law, contributed to their ultimate failure to elect him. But the Republicans' success has reminded us all that an effective field operation must look to the grass roots for its energy as much as its ideas.

Limits of Anti-Bushism

Kerry spent a lot of his time criticizing Bush's record. Through most of the campaign, he focused his attention on domestic failures—the economy, jobs, tax cuts, health care, energy—and toward the end he also attacked Bush's disastrous handling of the war in Iraq. Polls showed that the majority of voters agreed with many of Kerry's criticisms, and Bush's popularity numbers were low. One would have expected these attacks to stick.

As Teixeira pointed out, "Kerry never managed to convince many of the same voters who shared his criticisms of the Bush administration that he could and would do a better job in the areas he criticized."

Throughout the campaign there was abundant evidence that voters did not think Kerry had a clear plan for Iraq or, for that matter, for the country in general. His campaign notably lacked signature themes or proposals that typical voters could easily grasp and identify with. Does anyone seriously believe that voters knew or understood Kerry's plan for Iraq? For health care? For the economy? How many could recite the one or two thematic phrases (if they existed) that summarized what John Kerry stood for? It seems too many Americans suspected that Dale Carnegie was right: "Any fool can criticize, condemn, and complain—and most fools do."

The 527s as a group also underestimated the limits of anti-Bushism. ACT and the Media Fund raised more than $200 million to create their field operations during the election. But given the laws restricting them from advocating for any candidate, they could only oppose Bush. They could not use their clout to actively support Kerry or his policies. The resulting negative slant to their efforts probably helped sour voters' faith in Bush, but it did nothing to help persuade them that Kerry could do anything better.

Playing Dirty

When it comes to election tactics, a lot of people believe that the Republicans are smarter, better prepared, and tougher— they want it more. As David Morris wrote for AlterNet, conservatives view politics as war. The goal is to "demoralize and destroy the enemy, seize his territory and gain unconditional surrender." Liberals, on the other hand, "engage in politics as a contact sport." And in sports, "when the game ends, people shake hands and differences are set aside."

The Republicans of this era set no differences aside, before, during, or after the game. And the person who best personifies the "no holds barred" Republican personality is Bush's longtime advisor, main political operative, and evil genius Karl Rove.

As John Powers wrote:

Concerned only with preserving power, Karl Rove spent the last four years engaged in what pollster Pat Caddell once dubbed "the permanent campaign"—scripting every moment of Bush's presidency according to a political calculus. And what a calculus! Under his guidance, the Bush-Cheney campaign didn't fret about lying, pandering to the reactionary base, trashing its opponents' courage and patriotism, or polarizing America so deeply that half the country was sickened and infuriated by its own president. All that mattered was getting one more vote than his opponent. Rove got his win. Whether such politics could destroy America doesn't worry him at all. For in Wilde's famous words, he's the very embodiment of a cynic: He knows the price of everything and the value of nothing.

And so, in a way, Election 2004 should be a wake-up call for progressives. Among the major lessons to take from that debacle is that the gap between the Democratic establishment and its grass roots must be bridged; that the party must listen less to its consultants, pollsters, and insiders in Washington DC and more to its activists and rank-and-file base; and that it must nominate a candidate who can articulate a broader vision that Americans can identify with and not just a laundry list of criticisms of the Republicans and positions on issues.

And it is worth remembering that while more Americans voted for George W. Bush in 2004 than for any president before, it is also true that more Americans voted *against* George W. Bush than against any president in the nation's history.

Howard Dean is a physician and former governor of Vermont, and the newly elected chairman of the Democratic National Committee. He rewrote the book on how to run for president during his 2004 campaign. Using the Internet for unprecedented grassroots fund-raising and effective two-way communication with his supporters, Dean upended the pundits' and pollsters' dismissive predictions—for a time. After John Kerry won the primaries,

Interview with Howard Dean

Dean formed Democracy for America, with the aim of helping progressive candidates run for offices around the country. In February 2005, he took the reins of the DNC, where he is committed to further applying his bottom-up, grassroots approach. Don Hazen interviewed Dean in December 2004, before he started his campaign for DNC chair. Following Hazen's interview are questions posed to Dean by members of MoveOn.

HAZEN: What can we learn from what the conservatives have done to organize the Republican Party?

DEAN: Rob Stein has been showing an important PowerPoint presentation demonstrating how and why the Republicans' model is so effective. It is very convincing. The conservatives have very efficient coordination among the think tanks, the training institutes, their media messages, and their grassroots efforts. We don't do that. We have a lot of the infrastructure we need, but we don't coordinate. And despite some successes by America Coming Together, we are way behind the Republicans in the field. We had the best field organizing I can remember in this election. We had thousands in the streets in Ohio, but the Republicans had 14,000 homegrown people in the party doing the work there.

HAZEN: Yes, the Republicans have effective grass roots—churches, legion halls, gun clubs, chambers of commerce. What do you see on the Democratic side that can challenge the conservatives at the base?

DEAN: We can do the same as they do with unions, with more moderate churches, and [with] efforts like our Democracy for America, where we engaged people to run for office. We only raised about $5 to $6 million this time, but we can do much more. It's important to note that a bunch of our people who had never run for office before won.

People learned from a lot of the innovations in our campaign: we did the Internet, we blazed the trail for grassroots fund-raising. But the most important innovation is this: we learned to take ideas from the bottom—the grass roots—and to call on them for our ideas and actions during the campaign. The bottom-up approach. We had a conversation going with our supporters. That wasn't tried in the Kerry campaign. We truly learned from the grass roots of our campaign.

HAZEN: Can you give me an example of how that happened?
DEAN: The Meetups themselves [local gatherings organized on the Internet]. We didn't plan them, they planned us. My key staff person Kate O'Connor noticed this happening on the Web as a way to get people together. But it was started initially by people in the field. There were meetings in 850 different locations once a month. They were focused on how to get me elected. On the day after the election there were a number of Meetups. The Kerry people went. They needed a place to go and talk. They had just gotten clobbered in the election. In a sense, the Meetup model could do some of the things that the right-wing churches provide. They represent a place where people can go that creates community, and that gets people talking about common views and values. And by the way, the Meetups aren't progressive; they are reformist.

HAZEN: What's the distinction?
DEAN: What brings people together is not ideology. There are progressives as well as moderates, McCain Republicans, Greens, and even some evangelicals. They are united because they all feel the

need for change. The evangelicals are attracted because they see
the hypocrisy of the pro-life people who are pro-life only until the
child is born. They don't accept some of the teachings. They are
against gay bashing. Democracy for America has a powerful moral
attraction because we care about the lesser among us. Our movement can empower those people who have been left out of the
political process, like young people. We are all fighting the fact
that religious bigotry is back in favor, encouraged by the president.
Our organization encourages a lot of different kinds of people. We
show respect for differences.

HAZEN: The right wing has their religious fervor as the key organizing
principle. What is the Democrats' first principle—is it democracy?
DEAN: Democracy is part of it—clearly democracy is in danger. For
many conservatives, the end justifies the means, especially as we
watch how these partisan election officials and the secretaries of
state operate.

But in the end what will turn people on is empowerment, which
is part of personal responsibility. We can and we need to do that—
give people more responsibility at the local level instead of getting
bogged down.

Much of the right is an unruly mob. It is bound together by negative emotions and hate for people who are different from them.
We, on the other hand, support individuals for what they are as
individuals, as opposed to the right, which defines itself as what its
members are not. Our values are positive community values.

HAZEN: What about unions and the ideas Andy Stern is pushing to
revitalize the labor movement? His group, the Service Employees
International Union, was a big supporter of yours.
DEAN: Well, some unions are different from others. The union
movement has many of the same problems we've been talking
about. You have to go with renewal. Andy Stern understands that
we have to have change. He is a good friend and he is key. But I
also want to give John Sweeney a lot of credit. Sweeney began the

outreach to immigrants and low-wage workers. The labor movement needs economic and social justice.

HAZEN: Let's talk about the Democratic National Committee, and what should happen. Do you think that the DNC should control the state parties like they do in the RNC?

DEAN: No, I don't. In order to make good on the new empowerment, we have to genuinely give power to the states and grass roots. That's what we did in our campaign. I believe in order to have power, you have to give up power. I know that sounds Zen-like, but it is true. In order to get it back, in order for us to win, we have to empower the grass roots.

There is enormous angst right now in the Democratic Party among those who are running it, whose grip is slipping in the push toward decentralization.

Ultimately outsiders have to take over the party, and that is very painful for the insiders. But insiders can't make this work out. Power needs to come from the grass roots. The current Democratic Party is the old mode. You know, they say people go to see the psychiatrist when the pain of doing the same thing becomes more than the pain of changing. It is time to face the pain of change.

HAZEN: What was the single biggest lesson you took away from the 2004 election?

DEAN: Oddly enough, it is hope. We ran a better campaign in the field than I have ever seen. There is genuine difference out there, and we have to prosper by moving outside what have been our confines, by empowering people in the community. And I know that in giving up power some people are going to screw up, but that is part of the process—and progress. We really do have to believe. We are not automatons like the Republicans are. We don't take orders from on high.

The following questions were asked by MoveOn members shortly before Dean was elected DNC chair.

SYLVIA PINYAN, RETIRED TEACHER: What will you do to insure that all voters, in each state, have access to a universally transparent, accountable voting system?

DEAN: I intend to work with Members of Congress, the state Democratic parties, secretaries of state, the Democratic Governors' Association, other stakeholders, and the grass roots to ensure that every legitimate voter—regardless of their political affiliation—is able to vote, and have their vote counted. We must address the obstacles that voters in some locations faced this past November, like inadequate numbers of voting machines at certain polling locations, faulty electronic voting machines, and voting rolls that failed to include some properly registered voters' names. And critically, we must take steps to ensure the verifiability of all electronic voting. For instance, we need to use the referendum process (in states that allow this) to ban unverifiable voting machines and to protect voters from partisan secretaries of state.

TOM PETERS, COMMERCIAL FISHERMAN: What would be your list of "ideals," or things the Democratic Party stands for, and will fight for?

DEAN: Whether you call them ideals or moral values, there are a number of basic principles that I believe the Democratic Party should stand up and fight for. Here are a few: a livable wage is a moral value. Affordable health care is a moral value. A decent education is a moral value. A common sense foreign policy is a moral value. A healthy environment is a moral value. The feeling of community that comes from full participation in our democracy is a moral value. It is a moral value to make sure that we do not saddle our children and grandchildren with our debt.

ANNA SCHWARTZ, PHYSICIAN: What will be your strategy for sending the message that a progressive agenda is as much about "moral values" as is the Republican agenda, i.e., that economic justice and equality,

tolerance, civil rights, and environmental protection are ethical and moral matters?

DEAN: I believe that there are no red states or blue states, just American states. And I am confident that Americans will vote for Democrats in Texas, Mississippi, New Mexico, and Montana and all over the United States if we show up, knock on their doors, introduce ourselves, and tell them what we stand for. But we will not win by being "Republican-lite." Democrats must have the courage of our convictions. Every chance we get, Democrats need to stand up for what we believe in, frame the debate, and call for reform. Each time that we do this we drive home the point that our progressive agenda is right where the majority of Americans are. Because Democrats—not Republicans—are the party of fiscal responsibility, economic responsibility, social responsibility, civic responsibility, personal responsibility, and moral responsibility.

LYNN O'CONNELL, ADVERTISING: What is your plan for creating an effective Democratic message machine to clearly and powerfully present our point of view?

DEAN: I want to reform the Democratic Party and make it a truly national party. Improving the Democrats' message machine will be critical to our success. To drive home the point that we are where the majority of Americans are on the issues, we have to better integrate national and state party operations—the success of the former depends directly on the success of the latter. Two, taking a bottom-up approach to the development of the Party's message, we need to set core principles that define the Democratic Party and what we stand for. Three, the party must take advantage of cutting-edge Internet technology to fund-raise, organize, and communicate with our supporters. And four, we must strengthen our political institutions and leadership institutes to promote our leaders and our ideas. All of this won't be easy and it won't happen overnight. It will require exceptional cooperation between the national party and the state parties, unprecedented use of the grass roots, unparalleled message discipline, and significant financial support. But taking the White House and Congress and every other office back from George Bush and the Republicans will make all of our time and effort worth it.

LISA SCERBO, PHOTOGRAPHER: Many people like myself were energized during the 2004 presidential election. I volunteered to canvass neighborhoods and I made phone calls for Democratic candidates. I made my first financial contributions for a political cause. How are you going to keep people like me involved? Do you want to keep people like me involved?

DEAN: New supporters like you were the bright spots in the last election cycle. I intend to make the Democratic Party a truly national party by becoming competitive in every race, in every district, in every state and territory. We need you and other grassroots volunteers to stay involved. Our vision won't become a reality without your help. And we will keep you involved by building on our grassroots successes, expanding community-building initiatives like Meetups, and getting ordinary people to run for office. It is time we support all Democrats carrying the message of reform.

Interview with Arianna Huffington

Arianna Huffington is a writer and commentator who has written extensively—and with passion—about national politics. Her most recent book is *Fanatics and Fools: The Game Plan for Winning Back America*. Her column is published every week on AlterNet. Don Hazen interviewed Huffington by e-mail in January 2005.

HAZEN: How did the Democrats come to lose the 2004 election?

HUFFINGTON: It wasn't gay marriage that did the Democrats in; it was the fatal decision to make the pursuit of undecided voters the overarching strategy of the John Kerry campaign. This meant that at every turn the campaign chose caution over boldness so as not to offend the undecideds. Kerry's advisors were so obsessed with not upsetting America's fence-sitting voters they ended up driving the Kerry bandwagon straight over the edge of the Grand Canyon, where the candidate proclaimed that even if he knew then what we all know now—that there were no WMDs in Iraq—he still would have voted to authorize the use of force in Iraq.

HAZEN: How should he have been bold?

HUFFINGTON: The campaign should have been about big ideas, big decisions, and the very, very big differences between the world-views of John Kerry and George Bush—both on national security and [on] domestic priorities.

This timid, spineless, walking-on-eggshells strategy—with no central theme or moral vision—played right into the hands of the Bush-Cheney team's portrayal of Kerry as an unprincipled, equivocating flip-flopper who, in a time of war and national unease, stood for nothing other than his desire to become president.

HAZEN: But didn't Kerry clearly differentiate himself from Bush on Iraq in the debates?

HUFFINGTON: It was only after the polls started going south for Kerry, with the president opening a double-digit lead according to some surveys, that his campaign began to rethink its disastrous approach [to] Iraq. Once Kerry belatedly began taking on the president on the war on terror and the war on Iraq—"wrong war, wrong place, wrong time"—he started to prevail on what the president considered his unassailable turf. You would have thought that keeping up this line of attack day in and day out would have clearly emerged as the winning strategy—especially since the morning papers and the nightly news were filled with stories on the tragic events in Iraq, the CIA's no-al-Qaeda/Saddam-link report, and the Duelfer no-WMD report.

Instead, those in charge of the Kerry campaign allowed themselves to be mesmerized by polling and focus-group data, which convinced them that domestic issues like jobs and health care were the way to win. The Clintonistas who were having greater and greater sway over the campaign were convinced it was "the economy, stupid" all over again, which dovetailed perfectly with the beliefs of chief strategist Bob Shrum and campaign manager Mary Beth Cahill. But what worked for Clinton in the '90s completely failed Kerry in 2004, at a time of war, fear, and anxiety about more terrorist attacks.

HAZEN: But couldn't you make a strong case on the failures of economy? You yourself said they had Hoover-like job numbers.

HUFFINGTON: Yes, but even when it came to domestic issues, the message was tailored to the undecideds. Bolder, more passionate language that Kerry had used during the primary—like calling companies hiding their profits in tax shelters "the Benedict Arnolds of corporate America"—was dropped for fear of scaring off undecideds and Wall Street. Or was it Wall Street undecideds? Sure, Kerry spoke about Iraq until the end—how could he not?— but the majority of the speeches, press releases, and ads coming out of the campaign, including Kerry's radio address to the nation ten days before the election, were on domestic issues. The fact that Kerry lost in Ohio, which had seen 232,000 jobs evaporate and 114,000 people lose their health insurance during the Bush years, shows how wrong the polling data the campaign based its decisions on was.

HAZEN: But what about moral values? We're talking Iraq and security and jobs, but lots of people are talking about the values gap.

HUFFINGTON: Even Karl Rove, the "architect" of the president's evangelical strategy, says that security was this year's most galvanizing issue. But, ironically, however erroneously we got to it, the moral values debate is precisely the one Democrats need to be having right now. Because if they don't capture the moral high ground back from the Republicans, they'll never be able to capture the hearts and votes of Red America.

If the Democratic Party is not about bringing focus and urgency to the creation of a more fair, just—and, yes, moral—society, it might as well cease to exist. But Democrats can't get to the promised land by treating moral values as just another tactic their pollsters tell them they need to pursue, as something "we" need to figure out so we can convince "them" to vote for us. That's like an aging '60s rocker reluctantly trying on a white three-piece suit after *Saturday Night Fever* turned disco into a national phenomenon. Stayin' alive, indeed.

Reframing morality is all the more urgent because of what we can look forward to in the next four years of Bush.

Take the jaw-dropping federal debt, which currently stands at $4.3 trillion. The Government Accountability Office released a report at the end of 2004 that found that Bush's economic policies will have catastrophic consequences. And what was the administration's reaction to this frightening assessment? Vice President Cheney shrugged and announced that the administration wants another round of tax cuts. Basically a big f--- you.

Then there's our trade deficit, which ballooned to a record $165 billion in the third quarter of 2004. Thanks to this imbalance, America is racking up a staggering $665 billion in additional foreign debt every year—that's $5,500 for every U.S. household. Here is Bush's response to this daunting prospect: "People can buy

more United States products if they're worried about the trade
deficit." Sounds like he's really got it under control.

That said, it's not hard to see why Bush has hopped aboard the
Apocalypse Express. It offers him a political twofer: placating his
corporate donors while winning the hearts and votes of the true
believers who helped the president achieve a Second Coming of
his own. No small miracle, given his record.

**HAZEN: You have said that there is a need to rescue, resuscitate, rean-
imate, remake, rebrand, and redeem the Democratic Party. How can
the D's refashion, reinvent themselves for success in the future?**

HUFFINGTON: In 1992, the Republican Party found itself in very
much the same position as Democrats do today: out of power (with
the opposition controlling the White House and both houses of
Congress), lacking a compelling core message, and facing the
prospect of becoming what any number of pundits at the time
deemed—all together now—"a permanent minority party."

John Ashcroft, then governor of Missouri, wrote in the *Washington
Post*, "The Republican Party needs to shake itself loose from top-
down management, undergo a grassroots renewal and adopt a vig-
orous, positive agenda that flows from the priorities, views and values
of citizens who involve themselves in that process. . . . Our party
needs to frame its priorities more in terms of what we're for rather
than what we are against." These are precisely the sentiments now
being echoed throughout Democratic circles.

**HAZEN: That's an interesting historical analogy. But what about the
mechanics? How do you do it?**

HUFFINGTON: These days, with cable TV and the Internet working
24/7, getting to the tipping point can happen faster than ever.
With the right message and the right strategies, Democrats can
rapidly turn public opinion on its head, doing in 2006 what
Republicans did in 1994. But if they are going to achieve a simi-
larly spectacular reversal of fortune, the Democrats need to take a
page out of the GOP playbook and ignore all siren songs urging

them to lurch toward the victors. Instead, they must reclaim the party's true identity and return to the idealism, boldness, generosity of spirit, and core values that marked the presidencies of FDR and JFK, and the short-lived presidential campaign of Bobby Kennedy.

HAZEN: Okay, they shouldn't go to the center. I understand that. But in a lot of politics, the devil is in the details. . . .

HUFFINGTON: Yes, I agree, here are some practical steps.

Make sure that there is never another election held using electronic voting machines that don't leave a paper trail, or [with] voter suppression caused by long lines and not enough polling places in poor neighborhoods.

The D's should—to paraphrase Shakespeare—kill all the consultants, and while they're at it, do away with the bullheaded pollsters, too. The party needs to find and develop campaign teams that can run winning races in the twenty-first century, not keep rehiring the same professional losers election after election. Shouldn't there be an "eight strikes and you're out" rule?

Democrats also need to retool their party infrastructure. Conservatives have spent the better part of the last thirty years building a potent message machine—a network of think tanks, policy centers, and media outlets—that spends more than $300 million a year to promote its agenda. Democrats need to open their wallets and build their own well-funded message machine.

The Kerry campaign took in more than $82 million in online donations. Before that it was Dean. MoveOn was the pioneer. This combination of cyber savvy and sophisticated marketing must be used to help Democrats spread their message and build citizen participation.

The party needs to forge ahead with nascent efforts to recruit, train, and fund a better crop of candidates. As one film-director friend of mine put it, "It's ultimately about casting; I'm tired of voting for some guy who isn't right for the role but got the part anyway."

We must frame issues in strong moral terms. Why not start with the immoral behavior of giant drug companies such as Merck that continue to sacrifice the health of the public on the altar of higher and higher profits? According to Senate testimony given recently by Dr. David Graham, associate director for science and medicine in the FDA's Office of Drug Safety, as many as 55,000 patients may have died as a result of taking Vioxx. Shocking. But not to Merck, which had spent hundreds of millions of dollars convincing Americans to take its blockbuster pain pill even though the company's own studies showed that Vioxx greatly increases the risk of heart attacks and strokes.

If Democrats want to appeal to voters who believe in promoting what the president calls "a culture of life," they should make it a priority to put an end to the kind of corporate behavior that promotes a culture of death. Dr. Graham, while citing an additional five drugs that he feels pose a danger to the public, said that the nation's compromised drug oversight system had left Americans "virtually defenseless" against killer drugs and warned that we are facing "the single greatest drug safety catastrophe in the history of this country or the history of the world."

HAZEN: But who is the party? And how will you get them to do this?

HUFFINGTON: Twelve days before the election, James Carville stood in a Beverly Hills living room surrounded by two generations of Hollywood stars. After being introduced by Senator John Kerry's daughter, Alexandra, he told the room—confidently, almost cockily—that the election was in the bag.

"[If] we can't win this damn election," the advisor to the Kerry campaign said, "with a Democratic Party more unified than ever before, with us having raised as much money as the Republicans, with 55 percent of the country believing we're heading in the wrong direction, with our candidate having won all three debates, and with our side being more passionate about the outcome than theirs—if we can't win this one, then we can't win shit! And we need to completely rethink the Democratic Party."

Well, as it turns out, that's exactly what should be done. But Carville and his fellow architects of this latest Democratic defeat are not the ones to do it. A new generation of leaders needs to take a shot at moving the Democratic Party forward.

HAZEN: You mention in your writing about the Republicans that the Apocalypse is a factor in their thinking. Is it true that the fundamentalist view of the "End of Time" has some effect on the conservative economic policies?

HUFFINGTON: Absolutely, and nowhere is this mindset more prevalent than with the Bush policy makers at the White House, which is unwavering in its determination to ignore the future.

The evidence is overwhelming. Everywhere you look, it's IOUs passed on to future generations: record federal debt, record foreign debt, record budget deficits, record trade deficits. And this attempt to screw the future is not limited to economics. You see the same attitude when it comes to energy policy, health care, education, Social Security, and especially the environment—with the Bushies redoubling their efforts to make the world uninhabitable as fast as possible with their attempts to gut the Clean Air Act, gut the Clean Water Act, gut the Endangered Species Act, gut regulations limiting pollution from power plants.

HAZEN: Are you saying they purposefully don't seem to be worried about the future?

HUFFINGTON: Yes, that is the bigger problem. They don't see this as a problem. In fact, it actually all may be an essential part of the plan.

If [that] doesn't make a wit of sense to you, then you are clearly not one of the fifty million Americans who believe in some form of End-Time philosophy, an extreme evangelical theology that embraces the idea that we are fast approaching the end of the world, at which point Jesus will return and carry all true believers—living and dead—up to heaven ("the Rapture"), leaving all nonbelievers on earth to face hellfire and damnation ("the Tribulation").

Christ and his followers will then return to a divinely refurbished   31
Earth for a thousand-year reign of peace and love.

In other words, why worry about minor little details like clean
air, clean water, safe ports, and the safety net when Jesus is going
to give the world an "Extreme Makeover: Planet Edition" right
after he finishes putting Satan in his place once and for all?

November 3rd Theses

Adam Werbach was just 23 years **ADAM WERBACH**
old when he became president of the Sierra Club, one of the largest
environmental groups in the country. He then cofounded the Apollo
Alliance, an organization offering a bold, innovative plan for ending
our dependence on foreign oil. After John Kerry's loss, Werbach
wrote his "November 3rd Theses" and posted them on the door of
the Democratic National Committee headquarters in Washington
DC. The document then spread on the Internet, and Democrats in
forty-five U.S. cities volunteered
to post it on the doors of their
local Democratic headquarters.

> **"Insanity is doing the same
> thing over and over and
> expecting different results."
> —Benjamin Franklin**

I. The 2004 presidential election
was lost not by John Kerry over the last several months but by the
Democratic Party over the last several decades. Democrats have
lost control of all three branches of government for the foreseeable
future. We are now a minority party.

II. When the Senate Democratic leader is defeated while spending
$16 million attempting to get the majority of 500,000 votes, the
problem is not a lack of funding or effort.

III. The failure of the Democratic Party to connect with America's
desire for fulfillment is political death.

IV. Democrats are now history's spectators, Republicans its actors.

V. The obsession with denouncing the radical conservative project
as a "lie" has become a useful substitute for vision.

VI. Renovating Democratic politics is not a question of moving to
the right or talking more about religion. It is about creating a
framework that once again communicates to the core needs of the
American people.

VII. America is not now, and never was, simply "the economy, stupid." What the American people want is a deeper sense of personal meaning, a national mission, and passion in times of fear.

VIII. Returning the Democratic Party to majority status will require a political realignment no less sweeping than that which was accomplished by conservatives over the last 40 years.

IX. Only the breath of a serious and new moral-intellectual vision will be sufficient to resuscitate the Democratic Party.

X. Democratic candidates will continue to lose as long as they treat Americans as rational actors who vote their "self-interest" after weighing competing offers for health care, jobs, and security.

XI. Conservatives have spent the last 40 years getting clear about the values they represent. They have even developed a "family values" brand to represent a framework that coheres traditional prejudices around prayer in school, gun rights, restricting abortion, and restricting gay rights.

XII. By contrast, liberal or "progressive" groups and Democrats have spent the same period of time defining themselves against conservative values, even "morality" in general.

XIII. If resources continue to flow to the same leaders who have failed to construct a new vision and have thus left the Democratic Party in ruins[,] then we can expect more of the same. And worse.

XIV. Those who resist the process to create a new vision will be left behind.

XV. Candidates who intend to win should no longer hire consultants who repeatedly lose. Those who counsel caution when dealing with the indifferent, the disaffected, and the undecided do not understand American history. Consultants who advise their clients against offering a clear and compelling vision in fear that it will be attacked should find themselves without a home in the Democratic Party. The sooner they retire, the better.

XVI. Unconnected at a values level, the Democratic Party's laundry list of policy proposals is a confusing and alienating hodgepodge of special interests bound together by a vague sense that "we're all on the same side." Such a conflation demands no critical self-examination of the interest groups whose turf, and very identities, are treated as inviolable by Party chieftains.

XVII. The progressive vision must be a direct challenge to fundamentalism in all of its forms: political, religious and economic. It must match fundamentalism's power without replicating its authoritarianism. It must appeal to the values of liberty, equality, community, justice, unconditional love, shared prosperity, and ecological restoration, among many others.

XVIII. Democrats serious about returning to majority status must:
- Retire any leader who believes that we are currently on a winning path that simply needs more money and effort.
- Define and articulate a coherent set of values of our base, and be willing to lose those allies who do not share these values.
- Fight battles, win or lose, that define and advance our values and expand our political base.

XIX. In despair and defeat lie the seeds of triumph and victory. In that loss lies the opportunity to define a new progressive politics for the new century.

Interview with Adam Werbach

Adam Werbach is former president of the Sierra Club and cofounder of the Apollo Alliance. He penned the "November 3rd Theses," a clarion call for radical change in the Democratic establishment. Lakshmi Chaudhry interviewed Werbach in late November 2004.

CHAUDHRY: Why do you think the Democrats lost to Bush?

WERBACH: What we're seeing right now is denial from the leaders who are saying some combination of the following three things. First, they're saying we won the election, and that it may have been stolen. That's delusional. So, there's a lack of accountability there. Second, they're saying it was a mechanics problem . . . [because] we almost won. They think it's a matter of just a little bit of tweaking around the edges. And third, they're saying it was money. But this is the first election in my lifetime where we had a comparable amount of money to the Republicans, so I think it's specious to say that.

We must understand that the Democrats are now a minority party. Understand that we've been losing for a long time. We haven't won the majority popular vote since [Jimmy] Carter. Most important, we need to accept that the underlying moral-intellectual framework of the Democratic Party—liberalism—is dead.

I'm talking here of the Depression-era New Deal project, which Democrats championed, and that was liberalism. And it has been incredible. The liberal project created the minimum wage, the forty-hour workweek, Social Security. It was muscular militarily and ended fascism. It led toward civil rights. That's our heritage. But in my mind, it was betrayed in the late '70s and early '80s and at this point is a ghost. It's exhausted. *That* is the point of the election. And that is, in fact, more frightening.

The theory was that if we took all the Democratic interest groups and turned them out, if we took all the people who agreed with us on the issues, we would win. We turned out all those people and the interest groups—we still lost.

CHAUDHRY: One of your November 3 theses says that "the failure of the Democratic Party to connect with America's desire for fulfillment is political death." Is that why liberalism is dead?

WERBACH: Well, the liberal project was largely an economic project. It said people are rational economic actors, and if you give them survival-based services, they will vote for you. Most Americans today are not survival oriented; they're fulfillment oriented.

CHAUDHRY: In a sense, you're saying we are victims of our own success?

WERBACH: Yes, yes, that's well said. We have changed the circumstances for most Americans, and now we find ourselves unable to speak to them.

CHAUDHRY: So what is this desire for fulfillment now?

WERBACH: It's exactly what's going on, I imagine, in your life and my life, but we patronizingly believe that the people we advocate for don't have those same concerns. People are looking for something to believe in. They're looking for meaning in life. They're looking to be part of a broader project.

Democrats imagine the poor as an "other" and objectify their needs and wants and desires.

CHAUDHRY: As in, we imagine them as these poor struggling souls who are basically trying to make ends meet and put food on the dinner table . . .

WERBACH: Right before they go clean chimneys. It's patronizing. First of all, very few people define themselves as poor. Most people define themselves as middle class. And people who define themselves as poor, for example, suffer more from obesity than [from] starvation.

The way you hear this the most is that people voted against their self-interests. You hear that all the time. It exposes a defect in our thinking, which sees your self-interest as based on your economic status. It gives no credence to your fulfillment interest— this desire to believe in something.

CHAUDHRY: Your point is that we need to move toward a new vision that addresses what people need now rather than what people needed in the past—i.e., a basic level of economic support?

WERBACH: No doubt, some people still do need that kind of help, and I don't want to minimize their situation. But, yes, I think the majority of Americans are not looking for it the way they were looking for it during the Depression.

CHAUDHRY: But don't you think that we've seen the gap between rich and poor become incredibly huge? Things can only get worse with the Bush administration claiming a mandate.

WERBACH: Well, let me answer that in two ways. First, conservative economic policy hurts the people lowest down in the line, which creates more economic insecurity. When you're feeling economically insecure, you're going to look for something more to believe in. You're going to search more for faith. And who are you going to look toward? This faith-driven conservative movement.

Likewise, when you're scared because of terrorism and war, who are you going to look to? Conservatives. So the more scared you get, you look to conservatives. This is a positive feedback mechanism that they have set up.

It works the same way with the other liberal myth, which is that the conservatives are going to overreach. In this case, the more they overreach, the more they affirm that position. So they have a feedback mechanism for overreaching—that's what they're supposed to do right now. It's going to serve them better than not overreaching.

CHAUDHRY: So, progressives ultimately need to come up with a narrative, a vision, that addresses that insecurity and fear. So are you saying this is a battle we're not going to win?

WERBACH: If things get worse, people are not going to become economically more rational—that's the point. The fact that despair is increasing—and will continue to do so—is not going to lead to the rebirth in liberalism. That's not why [people] think that they've gotten this way, and it's not how they think they're going to get themselves out.

So you can't really address it directly. It's almost hackneyed to say it, but the antidote to fear is hope and opportunity. So we'll need to talk about hope and opportunity because those are the other important things that people believe in.

CHAUDHRY: Okay, so what is a core element of this new narrative?

WERBACH: Simply stated, a soul. When I talk about fulfillment, I'm really talking about something I want to believe in and fight for. It should be a powerful antidote to fundamentalism, be as powerful as fundamentalism is to people. It should be unchallengeable in the way liberalism was in the post-Depression era.

I see this as the winter of liberalism. We first need to accept that the liberal project is dead. We need to achieve that, so we leave space for something else to grow. Progressivism is almost just a placeholder for what hasn't been created yet.

Death is a very powerful experience, and out of it can come rebirth—all these wonderful opportunities. It's like we've been driving around with a dead body in the car for a while now. So the first thing really is to stop and kick it out. So I want not to jump past that. It's also sort of arrogant [for me] to assume that I can just roll off what those values are really quickly.

CHAUDHRY: So where does the Democratic Party fit into this? Does this model of focusing our energy and resources on a big national party organization have to be rethought?

WERBACH: Well, it does need to be rethought, although right now we don't really have that. The Sierra Club's annual budget is comparable to what the Democratic Party's annual budget is in non-election years. What you really have is power in the Democratic Party decentralized into these interest-group institutions—Sierra Club, NAACP, NARAL, ACLU—[that] organize people in what

we might call stovepipes rather than toward a single end, which is
to build political power.

It is similar to the intelligence failure [over the 9/11 attacks]. The FBI and the CIA each had their particular institutional goals that they were trying to reach, but they didn't reach their common goal, which was protecting America. They failed at their primary mission even while they were succeeding at their institutional missions. I think that's the same critique you can apply to Democratic interest groups, their single-issue and identity politics.

CHAUDHRY: So are you saying that we have to walk away from all that if we want to come up with a bold new vision?

WERBACH: That is central to the envisioning process. On a more fundamental level, that's how we're going to build political power.

For example, I've been trying to tell my friends at the Sierra Club that the most important battle for the Sierra Club in the next two years might be over public education. That is the battle line over collective activity, interdependence, the values we care about— much more so than the Arctic National Wildlife Refuge. That's a skirmish along the way that's not strategic. It's way off to the side.

James Dobson and Focus on the Family and all the evangelical groups believe they've won Social Security and a flat tax code at this point. Now they're going after public education. They don't believe that the government should be socializing Americans in nonreligious education. So they're trying to dismantle public education, which would have deep ramifications. Especially since we live in a market-based economy, where education is the only real guarantee of opportunity.

If you take away public education, you basically have a frozen class system, a caste system, all of a sudden. If you don't have public education, that is really the end of the social compact.

CHAUDHRY: Let's talk about the role of the government in other areas. Do you think that the traditional liberal idea of an interventionist government is one of the things we have to rethink?

WERBACH: Absolutely. And that's very difficult for me, having been a traditional environmentalist. It's just not working—the government doesn't have the capacity to do all the things that we want it to do. To my mind, bringing a more in-depth understanding of the commons is part of the answer. Common ownership is communal and has really very little to do with government. It may be needed to produce rules for commons management, but ultimately most commons will be managed by neighborhoods—a community of citizens and states—rather than necessarily being government mandated.

CHAUDHRY: You're talking about local self-government?

WERBACH: Local self-efficiency is part of it. Honest environmentalists have always understood that federal protection placed on local communities who don't like them is not a sustainable model. It may work if you're on a triage table, but ultimately you need to have a consensus that works for everyone.

CHAUDHRY: As the cofounder of the Apollo Alliance, do you believe that traditionally populist solutions—as in expanded government spending, punishing corporations, protectionism—are effective in dealing with something like outsourcing?

WERBACH: These are the hard questions that we need to answer before we can decide what the new values and policies look like. For example, if a job gets moved to India and someone in India now has an opportunity they never had before, is that necessarily a bad thing? Now, we might say [that] we need to deal with transitional industries in the United States and other such things. But to reflectively say outsourcing is bad is just simplistic and, truthfully, sort of jingoistic.

CHAUDHRY: The Apollo Alliance's solution would instead be to think more creatively about job creation here, right?

WERBACH: That's where I think local self-sufficiency comes in. At Apollo, we talked to a number of start-up solar companies, energy

companies. We need to find technology that can be built locally. 41
For example, wind turbines can't be shipped across oceans. The
turbines have to be made close to where they are actually going to
be installed. It actually decentralizes production, which is good.

CHAUDHRY: Right, and they create jobs in the local economy. What is
the role of government in this process?
WERBACH: The government could help make the market. In this
case, it could guarantee investment. We've been looking deeply at
Fannie Mae and what it does for home ownership. America is one
of the only countries [to] have a thirty-year mortgage—most countries have fifteen or ten. That increases home ownership in
America tremendously, and it increases individual personal wealth.
It was a government policy that created Fannie Mae. So we're
looking at what we'd call Effie Mae, as in an energy efficiency trust.

CHAUDHRY: What you've been describing is a radical transformation in
how liberals think about and do politics. How do we bring that about?
WERBACH: Let me give you an example. The Sierra Club needs to
see its goal as building political power that will eventually achieve
its environmental objectives. Not its first goal as being to achieve
its environmental objectives. Take the NRA. They go to pro-gun-
control districts and run ads on tax reform in, say, Colorado
because they know it will get their people the votes—and that's
fine with them.

The environmental movement, on the other hand, said nothing
about the war. How can any movement that claims to be a political movement say nothing about the war? Even though we know
that the [diplomatic] relationships that Bush was shredding are
exactly what we require for international cooperation on global
environmental problems.

CHAUDHRY: How do you think we ended up here, becoming just a
bunch of single-issue interest groups held together loosely by a larger
party?

WERBACH: This is a left-wing conspiracy. Foundations push toward this. The Democratic Party has always pushed this model. Each president has a labor liaison, an environment liaison, and so on. You then negotiate with these people to bring their little piece to the president, and the president says what to do. It's institutionalized in this way.

I'm most critical of environmentalism because it's where I come from, but we have a lot of money here, probably $2 or $3 billion a year. It's outrageous. And it doesn't really produce very much for that. Every global ecological indicator is tanking right now.

CHAUDHRY: So what should our strategy be for the next four years?
WERBACH: We should fight everything. An opposition party fights. An opposition party does not negotiate. Anyone who tries to negotiate right now should not be welcomed. I have made it very clear [that] any environmental leader who tries to negotiate a global warming deal in the next four years should bear the wrath of all of us. And there are people looking to do that. There are deals to be made, but they're all bad deals. You don't negotiate from a position of weakness, and we're in a position of weakness. So, the first thing is to fight. There's no reason to aid them in their quest.

CHAUDHRY: Or give them any excuse to look more moderate when they're not.
WERBACH: Right. So first thing is to fight, and the second is to provide bold solutions that may lose—that may lose badly. Let's say that the first $80,000 of everyone's income should be tax free. Let's offer to pay a mother and father to stay at home and raise their child. Let [the conservatives] fight against motherhood. They're cloaking themselves in motherhood, but they don't really care about mothers.

CHAUDHRY: So the point is not to be pragmatic anymore?
WERBACH: Exactly. At this moment, we're freed from reliance on the incrementalists.

We need to throw out the leaders who came in during the
Watergate era and have now outlived their usefulness. What
frightens me most are the deals they are willing to make. They
want to say they did something. All of a sudden there's all this
respect for "red" states. They're searching to make a compromise
to show that they can work together.

Finally, I'd say this: The liberal creed is "Don't mourn, organize."
For a moment, at least, we have to say, "It's time to mourn, not
organize." That is what is going to give us the power to build something really good.

Fear and Loathing: From 9/11/01 to 11/2/04

VIVIAN DENT

Vivian Dent is a psychotherapist in private practice in San Francisco.

As the Ohio results made it clear that George W. Bush had won reelection on November 2, 2004, a television network commentator remarked, "Fear won out over anger." It wasn't just the most important election in a generation, but also the most emotional. In this hothouse of feelings, the Republicans adroitly manipulated the politics of fear. Democrats, meanwhile, fumbled the politics of anger and failed to inspire the politics of courage and hope.

Like so much in this election, the fear that drove the Republican vote and the outrage that fueled so much progressive activism took root in the 2000 election and flourished after the 9/11 attacks. Aghast at the violence, death, and destruction, Americans looked to the White House to help us discover what kind of world we had entered. The Bush team responded with a series of choices that systematically reinforced the country's fear and dependency while undermining its hope and trust.

Bush quickly framed the U.S. response as a "war on terror," with himself in sole command. Then, with the full cooperation of the media, his administration repeated that frame so assiduously that many Americans quickly became unable to think of it in any other way. Nevertheless, many people commented, rightly, on how little the tools of war could actually do to counter the threat posed by small pockets of terrorists, operating outside the law, scattered in cities and countries around the globe. They noted that penetrating and destroying these cells would demand rigorous international police and intelligence efforts, involving both staunch allies and nations whose agendas were far less trustworthy.

44

But the words *war on terror* spoke clearly and directly to people   45
who were frightened and overwhelmed in the wake of the attacks.
War is about fighting, and people wanted to fight back. Fighting
back feels strong. Those who spoke for a more nuanced approach
never came up with language or a strategy that could compete
with this immediacy.

So the Bush frame prevailed. White House spokespeople then
extended the frame, making the war on terror "permanent." The
administration nurtured Americans' fears and passivity. It repeatedly issued vague "terror alerts" that created a sense of lurking
danger directors of horror flicks could envy.

The fear and dependency the administration cultivated found
fertile ground in the minds of many who ended up voting for the
sitting president. These voters already had a lot to be afraid of.
Their kids didn't seem to be getting much of an education.
Manufacturing jobs were continuing their steady move overseas,
and now service jobs had started to join them. Farms had failed
and local stores folded, replaced by anonymous corporations
offering low-wage jobs with minimal benefits.

So a glut of dangers, above and beyond the threat of terrorism,
converged to frighten a large number of voters in 2004. Bush
could pretty much have won on fear alone, according to Gary
Langer, director of polling at ABC News. He cited data revealing
that "forty-nine percent of voters said they trusted only
President Bush to handle terrorism, eighteen points more than
said they trusted only John Kerry. Among those who trust only
Bush to handle terrorism, ninety-seven percent, quite logically,
voted for him."

The Kerry campaign, by contrast, began by vastly underesti-
mating the importance of Iraq and the war on terror in the election, then compounded its mistake by ignoring the impact of fear
on people's minds, hearts, hopes, and dreams.

Fear narrows people's thinking, moves them away from logic
and toward emotional and physical reactions. Its effects start in
the brain; when they're too scared, people literally can't think

straight until they get some reassurance. Complex policies and nuanced arguments turn into noise that just confuses and upsets them more.

Frightened people are also *motivated* to cling to the familiar. What's familiar offers them comfort and security, a feeling of being at home. People who feel comfortably open-minded may be interested to learn that children raised by gay parents do just as well in life as those raised by heterosexual couples. Those who are hewing to familiar paths will experience ideas like this as threats to the only stability they have. They won't care about the truth-value of the evidence (although they may be reassured by convincing themselves that it's false). They will reject the idea viscerally, as an intrinsic menace.

And fear reinforces itself in groups. To the extent that its members do not believe they can solve their own problems, a fearful group often idealizes its leader as a savior or protector. Dependent on the leader for safety, the group cannot allow the possibility of learning anything that would undermine its faith, and so members ignore or deny ways that the leader actually has disappointed them. Information that could make them question the leader feels hateful, injurious. A person who confronts them with the leader's real or potential failings easily becomes the enemy, someone who by definition does not have their interests at heart.

For all of these reasons, a brainy, publicly unemotional candidate like John Kerry had his work cut out for him. He had to reach those voters through action and feeling, not just rational argument and sensible policies. His campaign never seemed to recognize this fact, however. The Kerry most Americans saw was an intense, ambitious, highly educated, and extraordinarily wealthy East Coast guy with a lot of words and a lot of policies. They never saw a man of passion.

This is ironic, given the genuine fury that the Bush administration had ignited in so many voters. Yet, apparently out of concerns over being labeled "negative," the Kerry campaign rarely tapped into the rage that most Americans (not just liberals) felt toward outright lies and unjust attacks, especially in the wake of 9/11. Again underplaying the role of emotion, however, the Kerry team never seemed to understand how much the election would hinge on Iraq and the war on terror.

If the Kerry campaign tried to sidestep the centrality of fear and anger, many liberals and progressives did not. They had a lot to be angry about. An unelected president, appointed by a 5–4 Supreme Court decision, had arrogantly pursued a radically conservative agenda—socially, economically, environmentally, and above all internationally. He had lied, repeatedly and apparently without scruple, to elected officials and to the public. He dismissed those who didn't agree with him, no matter how informed they were, and he seemed to be claiming divine inspiration for his decisions. He had led the country into what a growing number saw as a catastrophic war while failing to take the steps that many believed actually would protect us from attack. For all of these reasons, of course, a lot of people also feared Bush and his policies.

Before the primaries, the cry "Anyone but Bush" galvanized Democrats across the political spectrum. Kerry was nominated as the guy who could beat Bush, not as a man who inspired hopes and dreams. For perhaps the same reasons that he could not reach fearful voters, Kerry failed to fire people up and turn the story around—to make the campaign about electing him, not just about defeating Bush.

So liberals and progressives could tap into anger and fear—their loathing of Bush—far more readily than they could project enthusiasm about a future Kerry administration.

In retrospect, it seems that this anger and fear all too often translated itself into contempt—toward Bush, his people, his policies, and his supporters.

Contempt is pernicious because it so thoroughly alienates people from one another. Only raw hatred creates deeper chasms. Even furious people can fight things out and maybe in the process come to some new understanding. But once contempt takes hold, no one's left worth arguing with.

For those on the receiving end, contempt creates a hot, smoldering burn—and a ferocious desire to get their own back. Rush Limbaugh, Ann Coulter, Bill O'Reilly, and a whole lot of others owe their careers to this fact. But contempt ends up hurting the contemptuous as well. First, it destroys interest and faith in the other. When you feel scornful of someone, you stop being curious about what motivates them; you already "know" that it's ignorance, or greed, or prejudice, or some other stupid thing. Politically, this reaction creates major problems. From the Clinton/Lewinsky affair through the Janet Jackson flap, a lot of city people felt bewildered, even amused, at the fury that so many Americans were expressing. Okay, these things weren't great, but why the big fuss?

Assuming that the moral outrage came from a bunch of narrow-minded prudes seems to have left a lot of liberals regrettably incurious. Contempt can also shade into more subtly patronizing attitudes. Environmentalist Adam Werbach argues that liberals who emphasize economic issues often fall into this trap. "Most Americans today are not survival oriented; they're fulfillment oriented," says Werbach. "People are looking for something to believe in. They're looking for meaning in life. They're looking to be part of a broader project." Werbach believes that understanding people in economic terms vastly underestimates them. "Democrats imagine the poor as an 'other' and objectify their needs and wants and desires. . . . The way you hear this the most is that people voted against their self-interests. You hear that all the time. It exposes a defect in our thinking, which sees your self-interest as based on your economic status. It gives no credence to your fulfillment interest—this desire to believe in something."

Another, equally damaging effect of contempt is that it leads people to underestimate—and even denigrate—the enemy. Remember Metro vs. Retro? All those pictures of cool progressive types paired off against hopelessly unhip conservatives? In all our confidence about being at the leading edge of change, Democrats missed how successfully Republicans were painting themselves as the party of the future, with Democrats as the ones clinging to a lost dream. Bush repeatedly promised to "modernize" and "reform" Social Security. However much he obscured his own privatizing intentions, a lot of people apparently believed him when he portrayed Kerry's promises to maintain current benefits as living in the past. Likewise with terrorism and the war in Iraq: Bush managed to sidestep the content of Kerry's criticisms by accusing him of living in a pre-9/11 world. And, as union organizer Frank Joyce has explained, that left Democrats out of touch with the "universal perception that the world today is *different. Way different.*" Unions, Joyce says, recognize these tactics all too readily.

Looking at Bush through urban, progressive eyes, it seemed inconceivable that people really saw him as a beacon of hope, a man who could lead Americans into a better future. But a whole lot of folks were saying just that, and it took a certain hubris not to hear them.

So now we're looking at the future, working hard not to get trapped in our own disillusionment. Yes, conservatives and the media played into people's fears, reinforcing narrow-mindedness and blind conformity, and we have to hold them responsible for that as we develop our own more hopeful message for the future. At the same time, the mistakes of 2004 have a lot to teach us. To the extent that progressives have come to value logic *over* emotion, science *over* religion, we need to rediscover our ability to appreciate and speak to both sides. Sure, faith and emotion can be used to manipulate—but they can also inspire people to great acts.

A big reason we're progressives is that we care deeply about fairness, and that means making sure everyone's voice gets heard. In the last election, our assumptions deafened us to a group of voters who care about a lot of the same things we do. Our contempt alienated some more—and Bush won by only 3 percent. Many people who never think about policy share our values and feelings about how the world is changing, how we should help each other, what's just and unjust. We can reach them by touching their hearts.

Van Jones is executive director of the Ella Baker Center for Human Rights and a board member of the California Apollo Project, Bioneers, and the Rainforest Action Network. Immediately after the 2004 election, Jones wrote an e-mail that circulated widely around the nation. Amid the profound loss that progressives felt, Jones identified something hopeful: "Somehow we have hatched what looks like a genuine, cross-class, multi-racial, 'pro-democracy' movement—standing up to an increasingly authoritarian regime. And we did it all in about 18 months. We should be damned proud." Jones was interviewed in November 2004 by Terrance McNally, host of the radio show *Free Forum with Terry McNally* on KPFK 90.7 FM in Los Angeles.

Interview with Van Jones

MCNALLY: In your postelection essay, you claim you can see a vital pro-democracy movement. Can you clarify what that means to you? **JONES:** This was a very different election than 2000, where you had Democrats versus Republicans while many of the progressives supported [Ralph] Nader, either in their hearts or actively. In 2004 you had the Kerry campaign doing what it was doing, you had the Democratic Party doing what it was doing, and then you had this magnificent outpouring of decentralized disaggregated efforts— America Coming Together, National Voice, Count Every Vote, the League of Independent Voters, the Hip Hop Political Convention. You had this huge flowering from the grass roots of opposition to the Bush regime that was not a part of the Kerry campaign, not coordinated by the Democratic Party. It was alongside, under, and over all of that.

Its present form and expression is unprecedented. We may have seen elements of it before with the Rainbow Coalition, the civil rights movement, the antiwar movement, et cetera, but this present multiracial, multigenerational, cross-class unity against what the Bush administration is doing and its willingness to engage in electoral politics is a new development.

It's a very special character because it's not a black-led thing, it's not a woman-led thing. There's no particular identity group that you could point to as driving the process. That means that we have the opportunity to do things in the United States that have not been done before.

The vast majority of the people who took part in the effort to oust Bush in November were neophytes and newcomers to this whole process. Many of these people either had not been involved in politics at all or their involvement in public life had been neighborhood based or issue based, but not primarily electoral.

We had to learn what a 527 was, what 501c3s could do and what they couldn't do. We had to start from scratch, and still we came within 150,000 votes in Ohio of ousting Bush and delivering a devastating setback to his entire agenda.

It would have been much better had we won. We didn't win, but still, this was not a Walter Mondale wipeout—

MCNALLY: —or a Goldwater wipeout . . .

JONES: Right, or a Goldwater wipeout. . . . That lets you know that what we should be talking about now is the fact that we have 48 percent of the country who are opposed enough to George Bush's agenda to support a less than stellar candidate and to work hard and to put millions of small donations on the table. For the first time in memory the Democrats were competitive financially with Republicans, and by some measures [they] had more money than the GOP—not because of big donors or corporations, but because of ordinary people donating mostly online.

MCNALLY: At some point in the '80s the Democratic Party decided to fight the Republicans for corporate donations. That led to the dominance of the party by its very center-right corporate wing, the Democratic Leadership Council. But 2004 showed that the DLC's essential premise is no longer true, and that may be one of the powerful liberating forces of this election.

JONES: I think that's right. The question now I think is "Where do we go from here?"

You have the right wing that was out of power from FDR's New

Deal through Johnson's Great Society and beyond. Even when they were able to elect Reagan president twice, they didn't have the Congress and they didn't have the courts. Even when they had Newt Gingrich running Congress, they didn't have the presidency. Now they have all three branches of government.

We, however, have yet to be heard from. It's a mistake to think that liberals and progressives have been putting a hundred percent of our efforts into the electoral arena. In fact, most of us have just now said, "Okay, how do I get involved?"

What this means is that there are two new forces, two new dynamics: one, the small-donor online phenomenon, which frees up the Democratic Party from having to follow a pro-corporate vision of national politics, and two, this incredible vast treasure of people who know how to register voters, know how to raise money, know how to organize people, know how to do campaigns. They are now called into action in the electoral arena.

This may be the winter as far as the American left is concerned, but you can begin to see the spring, and you can begin to make out the outlines of the next left, the next progressive movement, both on the money side and on the talent side.

What you have now is a country where people in the so-called red states are angry, confused, frustrated. They know that things aren't going well. They've been told that they should blame the liberals for that. But the majority of the people in the South or the Midwest are not dyed-in-the-wool committed Bushites.

MCNALLY: You actually see the "red states" as fertile ground. . . .

JONES: I do, because, first of all, a progressive movement that's worthy of the name will not be locked into the cosmopolitan cultural regions. We have to imagine a progressive politics that works for the red states as well as the blue states. What we've got to do is, first of all, stop mocking the red states. Mocking the red states helps Bush and hurts us. We've got to give up the cheap pleasures of making fun of people. We can't lead a country we don't love. We can't lead people we don't love.

I'm from the rural South. I'm a Christian. I grew up in the church. I still go to church. And I'm so far left that if I were on the left side of Pluto, I'd be on a pogo stick trying to get further left.

One of the options that we have now is to make clear we're not going to fall into the false debates that the right wants us to have—in which we say "welfare state" and they say "warfare state," and folks think, "Well, we're at war, so we better go with the warfare state people."

We don't want the U.S. government to be a nanny, but we don't want it to be a big bully either. There is another role for the government, and that role is partner. We want the government to be a partner to ethical business, those people who are trying to do business the right way, who are honoring their workers and honoring the environment. They need to be given support through partnership with the government. And those businesses who are polluting everything and exploiting workers should get the stick.

MCNALLY: One thing I hear you saying is that the same kind of flawed thinking and flawed strategies that results in looking at the country as red and blue maybe looks at issues and entities as black and white.

JONES: Exactly. No ordinary people are either a hundred percent for labor or a hundred percent for business. People want to see others paid fairly. They want to make products that don't hurt people. People have a mix of concerns, and we should be speaking to that. We should be speaking to the best of American labor and the best of American business. We should be offering that as a meaningful alternative to the military-petroleum complex that is trying to pick war after war after war to drain our treasury and bankrupt the federal government. In other words, we can't let the right wing decide where the lines are.

When it comes to people of faith, we have to remember that the abolitionists were disproportionately people of faith. Quakers ran the Underground Railroad. The civil rights marchers who spilled their blood on the ground to spread the blessings of democracy marched out of churches. More recently, in the 1980s, the sanctuary movement in solidarity with the democracy movements of Latin and South America was led by churchfolk.

When we give right-wing fundamentalist bigots who are using religious symbols to disguise anti-woman, anti-state bigotry the courtesy of calling them "the religious people," we're doing them an enormous favor. No, we mustn't fall into that trap. We should be saying to them, "You're a microscopic minority of the communities of faith in this country, most of whom are on our side on economics, most of whom don't like war, most of whom long to see this country live out the better principles of Christianity and are disappointed when we don't."

As I wrote in that e-mail, our moment of truth did not come on November 2. Our moment of truth is today, now, in the aftermath, and in the choices we make going forward. And I know that we will choose wisely.

Progressive Victories EVAN DERKACZ

Evan Derkacz is an AlterNet associate editor and former media coordinator for *Tikkun* magazine.

There was more to Election 2004 than George W. Bush's victory—there were a lot of bright spots for progressives that never showed up on the radar of the mainstream media or its pundits. While it would be delusional and counterproductive to ignore the scope of the defeat, it would likewise be a recipe for ongoing failure to ignore the important successes—and what can be learned from them. Here is a sampling of the success stories from Election 2004:

••• Voters in Nevada and Florida upped the **federal minimum wage** by a dollar to $6.15 an hour. Despite intense opposition from pro-business groups—not to mention Florida Governor Jeb Bush's lobbying—71 percent of Floridians supported it. In Nevada, support was nearly as strong, at 68 percent. Take any county in either state—from the most rural and conservative to the most liberal and urban—and the initiatives received a majority of the vote.

••• The seven Democratic senators who voted **against the Iraq war** resolution all won reelection. The senators and their margins of victory:
Barbara Boxer (California), 58 to 38 percent;
Russ Feingold (Wisconsin), 55 to 44 percent;
Daniel Inouye (Hawaii), 76 to 21 percent;
Patrick Leahy (Vermont), 71 to 25 percent;
Barbara Mikulski (Maryland), 65 to 34 percent;
Patty Murray (Washington), 55 to 43 percent;
Ron Wyden (Oregon), 63 to 32 percent.

••• Democrats picked up forty **state-level seats** and took control of twice as many state legislative chambers as the Republicans, virtually erasing the GOP's substantial 2002 gains. Democrats retook the North Carolina house and now control both the house and the senate in that state. Democrats also won both of Colorado's chambers for the first time in forty-four years—in a state that voted for Bush 52 to 44 percent.

••• In **Montana**, where nearly three of every five voters supported Bush and two of every three voted to ban gay marriage, Democrats won the governor's office and the attorney general's office, took over the state senate by winning six seats, are within one seat of becoming a majority in the state house, and gained control of the state's main regulatory agency, the Public Service Commission. Montana voters also approved medical marijuana use by patients with a doctor's recommendation by a 62 to 38 percent margin.

••• While a majority of voters in the "red" states of **North Carolina** and **Nevada** supported their president, they also filled the gaping financial holes left by his No Child Left Behind education policy. In Nevada, voters required lawmakers to fund K–12 before funding anything else, while North Carolinians voted to put money collected from fines toward schools.

••• In **California**, voters went against the prevailing wisdom of the Bush tax cuts and raised taxes for those earning more than $1 million a year by 1 percent to expand mental health programs. Meanwhile, Maine voters opposed a cap on property taxes, and voters in five Florida counties, including Miami-Dade, voted to raise more tax revenue to pay for environmental protection measures.

- •• **David Soares,** who ran on both the Democratic and the Working Families Party ticket, was elected Albany County's new district attorney in New York. Soares ran on a bold platform explicitly opposed to New York State's infamous and cruel Rockefeller drug laws. What was assumed to be political suicide was, for a candidate with a bold and decisive message, a victory.

- •• In Dallas County, **Texas**, Bush won by 10,000 votes, but voters in the very same booths chose Democrat Lupe Valdez as its sheriff. Besides being a Democrat and a woman, Lupe is openly gay and Hispanic. Dallas County has never had a female, a Hispanic, or an openly gay sheriff.

- •• All eighteen of the **League of Conservation Voters'** "Environmental Champions" won. Of the league's "Dirty Dozen," four went down in flames. Of the eight congressional races into which significant LCV resources were invested, the LCV candidates won seven, including Ken Salazar of Colorado, who beat millionaire and antienvironmentalist Pete Coors by 3 percent.

- •• On the **"green grass"** front, basic initiatives (like marijuana decriminalization and/or medical use) succeeded locally in Oakland, California, and Columbia, Missouri. Bolder initiatives like full legalization or less restrictive medical-use laws were only narrowly defeated in Oregon and Alaska, setting records for popular support along the way—an astonishing trend in a nation weaned on DARE and the drug war.

Among the bright spots of Election 2004 was the election of David Soares as New York's Albany County's first African-American district attorney. Thirty-four-year-old Soares ran on a platform unapologetically opposed to the draconian "Rockefeller laws" enacted in 1973, which require, for example, that a minimum sentence of fifteen years to life be meted out for first-time possession of a narcotic. The laws cost New York $600 million annually and almost exclusively affect African-Americans and Latinos. Robin Templeton, the former executive director of the Right to Vote Campaign, interviewed Soares for AlterNet in November 2004.

Interview with David Soares

TEMPLETON: You were the outsider and the underdog. Were you surprised that you won?

SOARES: No, we put in the work. We didn't have the money but we had the people. Money allows you to reach people in sound bites. My campaign was door-to-door. We could really talk through things with people. And it worked.

TEMPLETON: Who was in the coalition that supported you?

SOARES: It was built up from people I'd already worked with when I was in the DA's office. I was assigned to deal with the most challenged areas in Albany. I had to build a coalition not for political purposes but for the purpose of public safety—teaching [people] how to hold agencies accountable. [The coalition] included churches, neighborhood associations, progressives, the drug treatment community—a rainbow of many preexisting coalitions.

TEMPLETON: How does your local victory differ from the Republicans' national victory?

SOARES: In my case, you had someone finally say, "Enough is enough—this is wrong." Someone who had every reason to continue on in the institution that was paying my mortgage and car payment like it was all okay. I think this resonated with people.

TEMPLETON: The media says that the Republicans won on moral values. Was there anything comparable in your race that made people vote for you?

SOARES: The inherent sense of unfairness in a system that's supposed to represent justice. We have this vision of justice—she . . . [has] her scales, her sword, and blinders. But the Rockefeller drug laws in their application violate all of that. The thing that my opponents don't see is that most people have a person in their family with either a drug or drinking problem; addiction isn't confined to a particular zip code.

TEMPLETON: What's your advice to the Democratic leadership?

SOARES: You cannot take people for granted. Demographics have shifted, but you still haven't gone back to the communities you've taken for granted for so long. Get back to your base; do not underestimate the power of the door-to-door campaign. Organizations that exist in your area that you may deem to have opposing views—look to them for the common views and [to] bring people in. Look at what brings people together. For me it was public safety.

TEMPLETON: Where did the Democratic leadership go wrong?

SOARES: America is a country where you'd like to believe that every person has a chance to make it. I'm proof of that. People still want to hear those stories and believe in America. But Kerry had no message that touched people's lives and gave them hope. Instead he just explained to people the allegations and charges levied on him by the Republicans. That's the reason he lost.

TEMPLETON: Where should the Democrats go from here? What issues should they prioritize?

SOARES: Unemployment. The Democrats talk about outsourcing. What is that? Be honest with people. Don't fluff the language. I don't know why Kerry even repeated the word *outsourcing*. Let the people who are looking to destroy the manufacturing base talk about outsourcing. You talk about layoffs and people losing their

jobs. People are willing to listen to a real message. You don't have
to massage it. We're at war. We're a more violent country now,
[and] I don't understand why you would fluff or be soft on that.

Use the appropriate language. Don't allow the other side to
make *liberal* a bad word. People say the word as if you're a leper;
don't let the other side determine the agenda. You can deliver
your own message; put it out there and don't continue to respond
to attacks. All Kerry did was explain, explain, explain when we
were all looking for something to hold on to.

Voters, Fighters, Citizens, Youth

ZACK PELTA-HELLER

Zack Pelta-Heller is a freelance writer who contributes frequently to AlterNet.

While the youth vote didn't deliver the 2004 election for John Kerry, as many hoped it would, the youth turnout was undeniably high. Despite what some pundits and mainstream media sources were quick to suggest in the wake of the election, the percentage of eligible 18- to 29-year-olds who voted was the highest it's been since the voting age was lowered to 18 in 1972.

This high turnout didn't just magically occur. Although the stakes were higher this year than they have been in the past few decades, more youths voted because it was what was asked—and at times demanded—of them. Countless massive efforts, from nonpartisan and partisan groups alike, were made to reach out to young people in the months leading up to the election.

The exit poll numbers speak for themselves: 21 million 18- to 29-year-olds voted on November 2. Voters under 30 favored Kerry over Bush 54 to 45 percent. But what cannot be tabulated is the profound impact that activist groups made in communities all across this country. More than simply registering voters, these organizations started a dialogue among young voters (and potential voters) that might have a lasting effect on the political future of this country.

"The natural next step," according to Ivan Frishberg of the New Voters Project, is "to keep the connection alive between the elected and the electors, and to build that connection around issues that are priorities for young people." The New Voters Project focused its grassroots efforts on six key states and successfully registered almost 450,000 18- to 24-year-olds. As for the fear that voter turnout could drop off, as it did after the 1992 election, Frishberg says, "The issues that made this an intense election are still here, and our experience is that many young people are not ready to skulk back to the shadows."

One organization that is not about to let young voters become disenchanted with the political process is the League of Pissed Off Voters. This group grew out of the mounting fervor leading up to the election and became a national organization made of smaller teams of local organizers.

"We had an issues-based agenda," said Naina Khanna, the League's national field director. "We wanted to make politics accessible to young people, to empower people by teaching them about issues that affect their communities." In order to determine which issues were of particular concern to voters, the League sent volunteers to survey their peers.

The local basis for the organization meant that the League could use the momentum of the presidential election to galvanize people to get involved closer to home. In many cases, the effects were tangible. In Portland, Maine, for example, the League mobilized a few thousand extra voters on Election Day, which enabled Green Party incumbent John Eder to keep his seat in the state senate by a slim margin of about five hundred votes. It's efforts like these that prove the potency of young progressives in the electoral process.

Khanna admitted that her voters were devastated by the results of the presidential election, but the League is looking to the long term. "We need a forty-year plan," Khanna stressed. "That's what the right had in this election. . . . The movement will continue, and we will keep supporting young voters locally to lobby and hold elected officials accountable." League members are also eager to remind people that their elected officials have a responsibility to them, regardless of whom they voted for.

The League of Pissed Off Voters has wasted no time in reenergizing in the months since the election. In late 2004 it held public hearings in Columbus, Ohio. Disappointed voters turned out in scores to tell their stories of Election Day voting difficulties. Khanna said that the weekend ended with a moving discussion on electoral reforms, but for her the most moving part was listening to people voice their support for the League for making voting accessible in the elections to come.

For many, voting was made more accessible this year, but the fight is not over. Music for America has vowed to make accessibility a chief concern in the coming years. Molly Moon Lewis, MfA's 25-year-old executive director, says that same-day registration must be allowed everywhere, and that MfA began registering voters again the day after the election at various concert venues. MfA took part in or organized 2,304 of the approximately 3,500 music and political events that occurred prior to the election. The organization hosted renowned groups like Death Cab for Cutie and the Beastie Boys as well as lesser-known and local bands. According to Lewis, the artists reached out to voters by "talking about real issues affecting people . . . talking about how unemployment sucked, or how young people don't like bans on gay marriage or were screwed out of jobs or benefits and social security, and how they're oppressed by drug laws strengthened through this Republican administration."

MfA was formed in 2003. The group registered 20,000 new voters and engaged over 45,000 youths in the political process by making them members of the MfA community. Of course, as partisan participants, these voters were initially deflated after November 2. "The day after the election," Lewis said, "e-mails [from MfA members] began pouring in, saying 'We've cried, we've kicked and screamed. We're ready to work.'"

Election
by the
Numbers

While some aspects of voting behavior in the 2004 election received a lot of media attention—evangelical voters and the importance of moral values, for instance—there were some interesting bright spots that did not garner much attention. These are worth looking at, if only because they might be useful in building a bigger and broader progressive movement. Here, we look at emerging trends among some demographic groups for which turnout was significantly higher on November 2, 2004, than in previous elections.

The Youth Vote

Jehmu Greene, president of Rock the Vote, has spent considerable time trying to get more young people involved in politics and more young people to the polls on Election Day. In 2004, the youth vote, especially among 18- to 24-year-olds, was much higher than in previous years. But Greene points out some interesting characteristics about young, first-time voters.

> When you look at the values of today's young people, you see that they are more tolerant of different cultures and lifestyles. The reality of their demographic is that they're more diverse—and they've grown up with a different understanding about diversity. I think it's very promising that this is the most tolerant and diverse generation this country has ever seen. And that, through the years— whether it's the impact they had on this election, or in 2008 or twenty years from now—is going to have a very significant impact on public policy.

We are in a time [when] there are so many issues that are presented as if they [were] polarized to the extreme. But you'll see a different political reality with this generation—where it's not so polarized from a partisan standpoint and not so polarized from a community, constituency stand-point. Both sides need to really appreciate and understand what that means, how they're going to engage this genera-tion. For Democrats it's about how they should really find ways of nurturing, including, and reaching out to young people as their base.

Here are some salient facts about the youth vote, courtesy of the Center for Information and Research on Civic Learning and Engagement (CIRCLE):

- •• Percentage of eligible 18- to 29-year-olds who voted in 2004: 53
- •• Percentage of eligible 18- to 24-year-olds who voted in 2000: 37
- •• Percentage of eligible 18- to 24-year-olds who voted in 2004: 42

- •• About 8 million of the under-30 voters, or 42%, voted for the first time. They represented 64% of the 13 million first-time voters.
- •• Voters under age 30 favored John Kerry over George W. Bush 54%–45%.
- •• On the issue of gay marriage, 41% of voters under age 30 favored it, compared to 25% of all voters.
- •• By twelve percentage points, voters under age 30 were more likely than older voters to identify them-selves as liberal.
- •• By ten percentage points, voters under age 30 were more likely to believe that "government should do more to solve problems."

••• Young voters (ages 18 to 29) are more diverse than older voters, according to the exit polls.

   •• 13% classified themselves as Hispanic/Latino, compared to 8% of the electorate as a whole.

   •• 15% self-identified as African-American, compared to 11% of all voters.

   •• 6% identified as gay, lesbian, or bisexual, compared to 3% of the whole electorate.

The Latino Vote

The most authoritative source for information on Latino voting behavior in the 2004 elections, the William C. Velasquez Institute (www.wcvi.org), is a nonpartisan, nonprofit Latino-oriented research and policy think tank with offices in San Antonio, Los Angeles, and Miami. The following are numbers based on exit polling by WCVI.

••• 65% of Latinos voted for John Kerry.

••• 33% of Latinos voted for George W. Bush.

••• 7.6 million Latinos voted, a record number that represents an increase of 1.6 million (27%) since 2000.

••• 18% of those who voted in 2004 registered to vote during 2003–2004.

••• 58% of those polled consider themselves Democrats.

••• 25% of those polled consider themselves Republicans.

••• 20% of Latino voters considered the economy their top issue.

••• 20% of Latino voters considered the Iraq war their top issue.

••• 9% considered abortion their top issue.

••• 9% considered the "war on terror" their top issue.

••• 3% considered immigration their top issue.

••• 2% considered gay marriage their top issue.

The Unmarried Women Vote

Chris Desser is project codirector of Women's Voices. Women Vote, a project to determine how to increase the share of unmarried women in the electorate. Desser believes increasing the number of unmarried women who vote would bode well for progressive causes. "Unmarried women and unmarried men are the largest pool of new progressive voters in this country," Desser says.

Despite the 7.5 million more unmarried women voters in the 2004 elections (compared to the 2000 elections), they are still underrepresented as a part of the electorate.

Unmarried women share a worldview of government engagement for the betterment of society and hold the progressive line on abortion and gay marriage. Unmarried women agree that the government needs to be more active in solving the nation's problems—particularly regarding health care, pay parity and education—while the electorate as a whole wants to see less government action.

••• Unmarried women constituted 23% of the 2004 electorate, compared to 19% in 2000.

••• Percentage of unmarried white women who voted for Kerry: 55%.

••• Increase in percentage of married women who voted for Bush in 2004 vs. 2000: 13%.

••• The marriage gap is larger than the gender gap— there's a thirteen-point difference between men and women compared to a thirty-nine-point difference between married and unmarried voters.

••• Nearly two-thirds (64%) of unmarried women said the country is headed in the wrong direction, versus slightly over half (51%) among voters overall and slightly over half (51%) of married women.

••• Unmarried women turned out strongly for Kerry, giving him 62% of their support.

•• Roughly 58% of unmarried women said they wanted to know from the candidates how they would make the economy and health care better for people.

•• Only 35% of unmarried women said they wanted to know from the candidates how they were going to make us safe.

Statistics compiled by Deanna Zandt, a Web-site design consultant and political arts activist in New York.

UNDERSTANDING THE RIGHT WING

2

The Conservative Message Machine Money Matrix DON HAZEN

Consider that the conservative political movement, which now has a hammerlock on every aspect of federal government, has a media message machine fed by more than eighty large nonprofit organizations—let's call them the Big Eighty—funded by a gaggle of right-wing family foundations and wealthy individuals to the tune of $400 million a year.

And the Big Eighty groups are just the "nonpartisan" 501(c)(3) groups. They do not include groups like the NRA and the anti-gay and anti-abortion groups, nor do they include the political action committees (PACs) or the 527 groups (so named for the section of the tax code they fall under), like the Swift Boat Veterans for Truth, which so effectively slammed John Kerry's campaign in 2004.

To get their message out, the conservatives have a powerful media empire that churns out and amplifies the message of the day—or the week—through a wide network of outlets and individuals, including Fox News, talk radio, Rush Limbaugh, Oliver North, and Ann Coulter, as well as religious broadcasters like Pat Robertson and his 700 Club. On the Web, it starts with townhall.com.

Fueling the conservative message machine with a steady flow of cash is a large group of wealthy individuals, including many who serve on the boards of the Big Eighty.

Rob Stein has brilliantly documented all of the above in "The

Conservative Message Machine Money Matrix," a PowerPoint presentation he has taken on the road across the country, preaching to progressives about the lessons that can be learned and the challenges that need to be overcome.

In the face of all that the conservatives have assembled, Stein is nevertheless still optimistic, in part based on what he saw as promising, unprecedented levels of collaboration among progressives leading up to the 2004 election. But he emphasizes that there is much to do. "We, of course, continue to have far more challenges than answers or enduring capacities," Stein says. "Indeed, everything that happened in 2003 to 2004 can best be described as a 'stirring,' not a solution. We have miles to go before we have built a strategic, coordinated, disciplined, and well-financed community of local, regional, and national organizations that collectively can mobilize a majority progressive constituency."

However, "progressives should not emulate what conservatives have done," says Stein, a former activist and chief of staff under Ron Brown at the Commerce Department in the Clinton administration. He continues:

> Conservatives have built remarkably successful institutions and strategic alliances in the twentieth century that presumably are consistent with their values and, we know, are effective in promoting their beliefs.
>
> Progressives have different values, this is the twenty-first century, the conservative infrastructure is in place and will continue to grow, and so we have to do it all differently. We must build from both the ground up and from the top down. We must be technologically sophisticated and new-media, narrowcast-savvy. We must build institutions capable of great flexibility to deal with the rapid pace of change in the world. We need a new generation of leaders able to integrate the local/global complexity of the world to manage our institutions in 2010, 2020, and beyond.

Since he left the Commerce Department, Stein has worked at the Democratic National Committee and has been a venture capitalist, specializing in women-owned businesses. His PowerPoint message is particularly aimed at educating people with power, influence, and money—the high-net-worth individuals who can provide the backing to build a progressive infrastructure. After two stunning electoral defeats and the virtual Republican dominance in Washington these days, Stein's message has acquired a new urgency.

Stein says he woke up the day after Election Day in 2002 and realized "we have a one-party state in this country." He decided to figure out how it all happened—how conservatives, despite a healthy majority of Americans being opposed to their platform and positions, managed to build an infrastructure and a message machine that is so effective and pervasive.

It Didn't Happen Overnight

The story of the conservative rise that Stein portrays begins back in the early 1970s, when there was panic among conservatives, especially in corporate boardrooms, that capitalism was under serious attack, and something drastic had to be done about it. The National Chamber of Commerce asked Lewis Powell, a former head of the American Bar Association and a member of eleven corporate boards, to write a blueprint of what had to be done. The result, says Stein, is one of the most prescient documents of our time. The memo lays out the framework, the goals, and the ingredients for the conservative revolution, a project that has gained momentum and power ever since. Two months after he penned the memo, then-President Richard M. Nixon appointed Powell, a Democrat, to the U.S. Supreme Court.

Powell told the conservatives that they needed to confront liberalism everywhere and needed a "scale of financing only available through a joint effort" focused on an array of principles including less government, lower taxes, deregulation, and challenging the left agenda everywhere. The conservative right, starting with seed money from the Coors Brewing family and Richard Mellon Scaife's publishing enterprise, moved forward to implement virtually every element of the Powell memo. It is a story of how the conservatives—in spite of political differences, ego, and competing priorities—were able to cooperate and develop a methodology that drives their issues and values relentlessly.

Starting with just a handful of groups, including the Heritage Foundation, in the early 1970s, the conservatives built a new generation of organizations—think tanks, media monitors, legal groups, and networking organizations—all driven by the same overarching values of free enterprise, individual freedoms, and limited government.

Stein describes how the message machine works. If Rush Limbaugh wants something on vouchers, it's immediately in his hands; if Fox News's Bill O'Reilly needs someone to talk about the "death tax," he has a guest from one of the think tanks. Stein estimates that 36,000 conservatives have been trained on values, issues, leadership, use of media, and agenda development. These are not the elected officials but rather the cadre of the conservative network. Stein figures that the core leaders of the Big Eighty groups he studied are about 2,000 people who make between $75,000 and $200,000 and have all been trained in the Leadership Institute.

The wealthy conservative families that have been the early bread and butter of the movement and continue their support are relatively well known at this point, and they include Scaife from Pittsburgh, Lynde and Harry Bradley from Milwaukee, Joseph Coors from Colorado, and Smith Richardson from North Carolina. Important networking goes on at the Philanthropy Roundtable, where right wing groups are showcased.

But the key today to keeping the message machine fed is what Stein calls the "investment banking matrix," which includes key conservatives like Grover Norquist, Paul Weyerich, and Irving Kristol, who raise, direct, and motivate. Stein estimates there are about 200 key people who invest an average of $250,000 a year, and about 135 of them also serve on the boards of the Big Eighty groups.

"Each of these groups [is] 'mission critical,' and they are [all] strategic, coordinated, motivated, and disciplined," says Stein, adding that the investment bankers monitor them closely.

And contrary to popular belief among progressives, the conservatives who are part of that machine are of various stripes—far right, neoconservative, libertarian, evangelical, et cetera. What makes them so successful is that they form strategic alliances around common issues they support.

Then there is the conservative media machine, which operated at full power to get George W. Bush reelected in 2004. Conservatives and their allies were able to magnify their message through a network of right-leaning TV and radio channels, including Rupert Murdoch's Fox News Channel, which provided Bush and Co. with a 24/7 campaign infomercial—for free. Here was a news network with more viewers than CNN and MSNBC combined, constantly repeating, often verbatim, the messages out of the White House and the Bush campaign.

More help for Bush came from the far-less-known religious broadcasters. "Under the radar screen, the Christian church community has created a formidable electronic media infrastructure and now plays a major role influencing public opinion," says Jeffrey Chester, executive director of the Center for Digital Democracy. The religious media are producing and distributing "news," commentary, and cultural guides, and their reach and influence are undeniable.

As veteran investigative reporter Robert Parry argues, Bush's electoral victory proved that the conservatives have achieved dominance over the flow of information to the American people—so much so that even a well-run Democratic campaign stands virtually no chance for national success without major changes in the media system. "The outcome of Election 2004 highlights perhaps the greatest failure of the Democratic/liberal side in American politics: a refusal to invest in the development of a comparable system for distributing information that can counter the right's potent media infrastructure," according to Parry. "Democrats and liberals have refused to learn from the lessons of the Republican/conservative success."

The Road Ahead

Now, for the audience hearing Stein's presentation—in the face of such devastating information, and the power of the conservative juggernaut—one might expect that paralysis and depression would set in. But in fact the opposite has been happening. The problem is being named. It is visible, concrete; it makes people angry and then determined to act.

And, says Stein, there are "very important lessons" to be learned from the conservative experience over the past forty years. For starters, progressives must learn to find common ground and set aside some differences they may have. "A movement is built upon 'marriages of convenience' among disparate, but interrelated, strains of a broad coalition [that] is able to agree upon some core values," Stein believes. "It is okay for there to be disagreement within the family; not everyone will be equally interested in the same set of issues."

Citing the example of the Apollo Alliance, Stein says progressive groups "must develop well-managed, highly effective, issue-focused strategic alliances that transcend their institutional egos and their competitive instincts."

Stein sees reason for hope, citing the progressive momentum and energy evident during the 2004 presidential campaign in groups like the Center for American Progress, AmericaVotes, America Coming Together (ACT), and the Campaign for America's Future.

"However one evaluates the actual performance of these initiatives—and obviously they all have strengths and weaknesses—they represent a new breed of collaborative enterprise," says Stein. "Air America, Democracy Radio, and Media Matters are also important new beginnings. And this is all happening because a highly energized, more strategic community of high-net-worth individuals made significant new financial commitments to all of these enterprises. This is exceedingly hopeful."

But Stein is a realist as well and believes change will not happen overnight.

"Our major obstacles are atomization, balkanization, and minimalization of our grassroots and national groups, our donors, and our political operations," he adds. "We have very few effective strategic alliances among existing organizations—[although there are] more this time electorally than ever before—very few organizations with the scale necessary to make a major impact; too few passionately progressive, politically motivated individual donors who know one another and work together; lack of long-term strategic thinking; and lack of appropriate and necessary coordination and discipline, to name a few."

Nevertheless, the progressive community has a major asset base, developed in part during the 2004 election, with a good number of donors—at least fifty of whom have given at the $1 million to $10 million level—including a small gaggle of billionaires. The impact of Stein's PowerPoint, in an ironic way, is a good sign, because it gives people, especially donors, a handle on what is needed to move forward.

"A movement must have a diversified funding base of small, medium, and large donors," Stein says. "The large donors must have the following attributes: be passionately progressive [and] intellectually curious, want to be operationally involved in the organizations they fund, [be] willing to work and learn together as a community of donors, [and] be willing to write very large checks every year to the groups they fund and encourage their family and friends to also invest."

There are a lot of eyes on Stein as he moves forward to build a deeper, more dependable funding base for progressive infrastructure. Stein's effort is called the Democracy Alliance. He describes it as a network of high-net-worth individuals committed to promoting progressive ideals by investing in strategic, long-term local, regional, and national capacity building.

One donor who sits on the board of a progressive foundation and has heard the Stein rap is worried that the top-down nature of things so painfully obvious in the 2004 election could be perpetuated by Stein and other funding efforts like those of billionaires like George Soros and Peter Lewis. "It is so important to get resources down to the grass roots," says the donor, who wished to remain anonymous. "One of the major failings of these big donors meeting with [one another] and deciding where all the money should go is they reinforce each other. Where is the fresh thinking? They think one big idea should get all the money or one or two leaders should be the gatekeepers. That is not going to work. Putting all that money in the ACT basket certainly didn't do the trick in the past election, nor will giving it all to Podesta and Center for American Progress help build progressive infrastructure at the local level where it is needed, particularly outside of the Democratic Party."

To his credit, Stein says quite clearly that top-down and bottom-up strategies together are essential for future progressive success. Only time will tell whether he and his donors are prepared to let go of some of the controls, really get the money out of Washington, and let some roots grow at the local level.

George Lakoff is a professor of cognitive science and linguistics at the University of California, Berkeley, and a founding senior fellow at the Rockridge Institute. Lakoff is the author of many books, including *Don't Think of an Elephant!: Know Your Values and Frame the Debate* and *Moral Politics: How Liberals and Conservatives Think*. This interview was conducted for AlterNet in December 2004 by Chelsea Green Publishing editor Jennifer Nix.

Interview with George Lakoff

NIX: What do you believe to be the biggest lessons of Election 2004, lessons that progressives can make use of?

LAKOFF: One lesson is that Kerry needed to answer the flip-flop charge from the very beginning. Progressives need to learn that you absolutely cannot let the other side get a foothold and frame you in their terms.

Kerry needed to frame and attack George W. Bush about his lack of honesty and character. And the way to do that would have been from the beginning. He should have talked about all the ways Bush has betrayed the American people's trust. At the same time, Kerry needed to characterize his own vision in a way that made it clear that he had single positions on every issue. He should have crafted his message, said it briefly, and said it over and over again. Many of Kerry's problems stem from this one problem of not defining his message until it was too late, and allowing the other side to frame him in various ways. You cannot be on the defensive.

The biggest lesson, though, is that Democrats and progressives must stop letting the other side define and characterize them—on every issue. The reason the Kerry campaign allowed this was that their polls told them that the people don't like negative campaigning. It was foolish to listen to that. You cannot be quiet while they make you out to be a villain. You have to find the ways to explain the positive attributes of your candidate, while you campaign negatively about the other candidate.

NIX: Democrats and progressives seem to find negative campaigning distasteful and like to think that they can be all positive all the time and win votes.

LAKOFF: And they will keep losing as long as they believe that. I mean negative campaigning in the sense of pointing out all the true and truly bad things about the other candidate. There were plenty of true, negative aspects to point out about Bush—and not just related to jobs. This is not about smearing someone with untrue accusations—which I'm not convinced the other side is unwilling to do—but I'm talking about telling the hard truths, and telling them often. Defining the other candidate before they can define you. That's another big lesson for progressives and Democrats to learn. You need to start predicting and preempting how the other side intends to define you, and answer those charges immediately. Come out proactively. Never defend. Always be on the offensive.

NIX: So this is the point we've reached in politics: you must be negative, and you must figure out how the other side will be negative about your candidate and beat them to the pass?

LAKOFF: Yes, we've reached that point in politics. There are no neutral questions or issues anymore. Politics quite simply have caught up with the way the mind works. However—and this is important—journalism has not. Journalism has not found the way to deal with what politics has become. I see this with professional journalists, and I see it in the journalism schools. Students do not have the resources. They're shocked and dismayed by what politics has become. They want to deny or ignore it or feel depressed. But it's only depressing if you try in vain to hold on to an old view of what the mind is. The media have to be completely retrained. The notion of framing, how deeply we hold frames, has to be understood. You cannot get beyond frames. Again, there are no neutral questions or issues anymore, and this fundamental lesson has to seep into media coverage of politics. You can't have one side understanding this— the conservatives—and the other side—progressives—ignoring it, and the media not even understanding what's going on.

NIX: Can you give an example of the media not understanding what's going on?

LAKOFF: A producer from a National Public Radio show *On the Media* called me up recently to tell me that [a style manual] . . . many journalists around the country call on when writing their stories is dictating that journalists stop using the word *fetus* and replace it with the term *unborn child*. This producer asked me if I thought this was political, and when I said, "Of course it's political," she debated me. We've heard this phrase *unborn child* so much that it's physically changing our brains. Also, the word *fetus* has been demonized, even though it is a technical, scientific term. The right is so successfully framing this issue that a term representing a political agenda is becoming the "neutral" or "objective" word that journalists are supposed to use in their stories.

The right has been on this for the last forty years; they understand and pay attention to the way the mind works. They play the journalists right now. Many times, journalists don't even know that they are promoting the right's language. They see it as neutral and repeat it over and over—"tax relief," "partial-birth abortion." The right has come up with a whole list of values and language about those values, so that their spokespeople can use it over and over again and get the media to use their language over and over again, and to ask *their* questions. Until we hear it all so much, have it reinforced in so many ways, that it physically changes our brains. There is nothing neutral or objective about that. People talk about a "competitive marketplace of ideas." The notion that there are all these equally weighted, neutral ideas floating about out there, from which people will choose their views and opinions. It doesn't exist. The right figured out how to physically change our brains, and the left is only beginning to recognize this very basic fact of cognitive science.

NIX: What can progressives start doing today to build on this recognition?

LAKOFF: At a minimum, Democrats and progressives must figure out how to get the media to ask *their* questions. They must have the press using *their* language. And the only way to have that happen is to know what your values are, know what your message is, and have a whole list of words to use when talking about your values. So that a network of people can constantly be using this language. Democrats everywhere have to start using the same language. On the right, they've had Frank Luntz and others teaching them about language for years. They have schools for conservatives to attend. Over the last ten years, the conservatives have trained roughly 36,000 people in language, messaging, and using the media to talk about their values.

So progressives need, first, to come together and determine what they have in common and create a positive narrative about their vision for America. Kerry said he had values, but he never stated them. Can you think of one specific value that Kerry said he holds? People vote their identities and their values, not their economic self-interests. If you don't have a clear, positive identity and values that people can relate to, you do not have a chance. And progressives need to realize that elections aren't decided in the last months or year before the vote. The 2008 presidential campaign started on November 3, 2004, and the work of coming together, defining our values, creating the messaging, and using our language must begin in earnest right now.

NIX: But what about the wedge issues that reportedly brought people out to the polls—gay marriage, abortion?

LAKOFF: This is a tricky distinction. But conservatives found the ways to activate their base, those that adhere to a "strict father" worldview. These were not just issues, as Democrats understood them. They were, in fact, strategic issues, symbolic of values and identity. If you adhere to the strict-father, conservative view of the world, then abortion and gay marriage are dangerous, personal assaults on your identity and your way of life. Conservatives understood that it's not just about issues, but about what those issues stand for.

Also, Democrats have too narrow a view of what [the term]

moral values means. When the exit polls showed that 22 percent of the voters said that moral values were the biggest reason that got them to the polls, Democrats and the media accepted the frame that moral values are about gay marriage and abortion values. They need to understand that moral values are a much deeper thing, a whole worldview. And Democrats have moral values. They just need to name them and use effective language over and over again to have them brought into political discourse.

NIX: You've said before that the Kerry campaign's inept attempts at church organizing should be a major lesson. How can we put forth our religious values when conservatives have framed us for so long as being without them?

LAKOFF: There are a great many more liberal Christians in this country than there are fundamentalist, evangelical Christians, but they don't understand their common theology and what makes them liberal. The work that needs to be done—and is starting to be done—on this front is the study of all these different liberal Christian sects and groups and determining what they have in common so that they can join forces and work together. This was done on the right, and it needs to happen with churches on the left. A narrative will grow out of that research and outreach, and the reframing can then begin. As a party, we'll need to get them talking about what unites them, what activates their "nurturant parent" side.

After that, it's the same basic organizational work that needs to be done across the board. We can't expect to match the number of institutions, the think tanks, and [the] dollars involved in the infrastructure that the right has built over the last forty years. We don't have to, either. We must match their functions, though. We need to match their language, match their training for how they manipulate the media. We must all understand framing and reframing, and we must test and retest our frames. We need to organize on campuses, [in] churches, and around child-rearing ini-tiatives. People on the left discount that, but look at what James

Dobson has done in the way of creating a system for how you raise conservatives from the cradle. We need our own wedge issues [and] slippery-slope, multifaceted initiatives. We need to start building on the idea of being the party of ethical business, creating a moral economy, and being forward thinking about energy issues. We need to take back the notion of "life" and have a true pro-child initiative, one with pre- and postnatal care, health care for all children, sex education. And we need to be able to start talking about our own moral vision for America.

NIX: When did Democratic leaders stop being able to communicate effectively about our moral vision?
LAKOFF: I think it was 1968. I think our moral vision was assassinated along with Martin Luther King Jr. and Bobby Kennedy. I think we've been afraid to talk about moral vision ever since. And this coincided with a massive level of organizing and strategizing on the right after the Goldwater defeat.

NIX: So, we have nearly forty years of the right stepping up and the left side-stepping the issue of moral vision. How long, realistically, do you think it will take for Democrats and progressives to create anything like the robust infrastructure—the money and message machine—that conservatives currently enjoy?
LAKOFF: If we get at it right now, perhaps as little as five to ten years. But we need to be coordinated. And we have to let go of our belief that the facts will set us free. We need to come to grips with the reality of framing. There was this feeling in the '60s that if we set everything right once, it would be right forever. That is not true. It's going to be a constant debate, an ongoing battle that each side sees as good versus evil. It worked for progressives and Democrats to believe in the old ways, while the other side was not organized. But now they have the money and the institutions in place to do major battle and fight for their agenda. We need to identify the gaps in our system and get on with building what we need.

People on the left need to understand that they can't live their lives free of politics. Politics infuse everything, from our religion to how we raise our kids to what we think of our neighbors and what they should and should not be allowed to do. Life is politics, and we need to be organized and coordinated around a vision of what we think an American life should be.

Robert Greenwald is a documentary filmmaker and pro-
ducer whose works include *Outfoxed: Rupert Murdoch's
War on Journalism, Unprecedented: The 2000 Presidential
Election*, and *Uncovered:*

Interview with Robert Greenwald

The Truth about the Iraq War.
He is also a board member
of the Independent Media
Institute, the parent organi-
zation for AlterNet. Don Hazen interviewed
Greenwald in November 2004.

HAZEN: The conservatives have an effective grassroots
network. What are the best opportunities for progressives to build the
grass roots? What kind of media can help local successes?

GREENWALD: We can build grass roots by building independent
media. We are at a very explosive stage right now. The number of
ways and opportunities to use independent media, as exemplified
by the Internet and by advanced DVD film releases—they have
opened up the possibilities for more people to be reached on an
ongoing basis. I am in the midst of reading *We the Media* by Dan
Gillmor. *We the Media* is changing my thinking. For example,
Gillmor predicts that what happened to print media in the '90s
with [the onset of the] Internet will happen to visual media in this
decade. It is a critically important book for progressives to read,
digest, and act on.

HAZEN: What can you tell us about the impact of *Outfoxed*? How have
the movie and the campaign done?

GREENWALD: The success of *Outfoxed* has been truly amazing.
From the number of articles appearing about it to the sheer
number of people who have bought it and shown it to their
friends, it's been striking. The film allowed for a discussion of
Fox News that had never taken place because it is a so-called
news organization. Others were either afraid to be critical or
concerned about criticizing a competitor, or [they were] playing
by the rules of the club.

I am starting a new media company to continue the work that
has begun, using alternative media to reach a wide and growing

audience, with the films married to groups working for social change and looking at the films as means to organize, rather than something to have an opening weekend with.

HAZEN: What is the most important lesson of the 2004 election?

GREENWALD: The most important lesson is that we have a lot of work to do. We may disagree about the nature of the work, but there's absolutely no question that we've got a big and long job ahead of us. We have to look at it as long-term work. We cannot continue to look at it as [though] any individual candidate is going to suddenly solve our problems. We will win some, but the work will not be over. On a going-forward basis, we need to frame our campaigns knowing that it is a long struggle, so that we are not devastated. There may be a loss or two for us, but we must realize, in fact, that we are part of the larger long-term battle. Individual battles and elections must be looked at as part of the overall battle for social justice, not as endgames or be-all [and] end-alls. . . .

HAZEN: What would you do to change the political dynamic in this country? Would you try to take over the Democratic Party?

GREENWALD: Well, first, we are going to have to work hard, work obsessively and endlessly, and do it smart. As for the Democratic Party, yes, progressives must get in there and fight for its soul. This is a change for me. In the past I felt that electoral politics in general were irrelevant to social activism and social change. I no longer believe that. After my involvement with MoveOn and Progressive Majority, I am increasingly seeing the dynamic possibilities for taking over and changing the Democratic Party.

HAZEN: What do you think the progressives' strengths and weaknesses are today?

GREENWALD: Progressives have truly come alive, showing we are smart [and] creative and [have] increasing flexibility. Losing is a way to take stock. And having just seen a lost election, I am encouraged by the level of examination, with no sacred cows, in terms of ways that we need to be moving forward. I am equally concerned, however, that what we stand for shouldn't be changed and altered, given the ebb and flow of politics. Progressives have a strong core belief system—we need to find better ways to articulate that—but we must absolutely remain true and clear to that core system. When we talk of moving to the center, it seems we don't believe in anything but winning, and it also happens to be a recipe for failure.

HAZEN: How can we build more effective media for progressive ideas and success stories? How can the messages get out more regularly to larger audiences to enable a Democrat—or even a progressive Democrat—to get elected in this country?

GREENWALD: We can build more effective media by focusing on the things that Gillmor talks about, embracing ideas in the *Cluetrain Manifesto*, not waiting for gatekeepers to give us permission. The success I had with *Outfoxed* came in a big part because AlterNet, Buzzflash, MoveOn, *The Nation*, Center for American Progress, Common Cause, and others were not waiting for us to develop a marketing plan, going the normal route. They all grabbed the opportunity and ran with it. It's about creating new ways of reaching larger numbers of people, using that creativity that we have an abundance of, while at the same time keeping the pressure on through traditional routes—through the FCC and our politicians.

There are some phenomenal new opportunities for me as a filmmaker making use of new technologies. I'm planning to engage activists and filmmakers in supporting and marketing our films using viral communications and giving people a way to invest in the process and the result. I want people to truly participate in the making and distribution of our films in new ways that have never been tried before.

HAZEN: What are some examples from the books you mentioned that progressives could employ?

GREENWALD: From *Cluetrain*, the notion that the Internet is not a lecture but a conversation has opened up my eyes and ears and given me a new lens to look at this tool. It's given me a bunch of ideas that I will utilize in my new media company and with new films.

In Gillmor's book, it's a similar theme—the idea of transforming journalism as lecture to journalism as seminar or conversation. If you break the mold in your mind, the new ideas flow. He of course refers to *Cluetrain*. I am fascinated with possibilities for RSS feeds [free headline and summary content from Web sites with links back to full-text articles] as a way to accumulate and look at what an individual is interested in—kind of a "TiVo of the Internet" around subject matter.

HAZEN: Sinclair Broadcasting also was very controversial during the election, and now there is a campaign being organized to challenge [its] coverage. What is the campaign about? How can it be successful?

GREENWALD: The campaign against Sinclair is a very specific, targeted campaign [that] allows us to call attention to [the company's] bias in a totally understandable fashion for the general public. Sinclair has a show called *The Point* that provides a totally biased, one-sided account of the world every night during newscasts. These are public airwaves. [Sinclair has] an obligation to the public to provide a range of opinions, not just right-wing screeds. Sinclair is the largest owner of TV stations in the country, with many of them in the heartland where activists on the coasts and in liberal cities don't see [its broadcasts]. This isn't cable TV, where the ground rules are a little different and people pay for the services. This is network TV. So we created a place for progressives to respond. There's a good way to get involved—by writing or calling Sinclair's sponsors, and telling them what you want to see. And [this has happened] at a time where there's been a tremendous desire among people to want to do something.

HAZEN: Anything I didn't ask that you want people to know about?

GREENWALD: Oh yeah. One of the exciting things with *Uncovered* and *Outfoxed* was making use of my commercial filmmaking background and experience in presenting the films. I was able to build a model of an opening day and was able to have MoveOn, *The Nation*, AlterNet, [and the] Center for American Progress all screen the film on the same day. We got cooperation of the various groups working together and got much better coverage that way, because it had the markings of a traditional opening day for film, but we used a nontraditional media to create that opening. So it was in my mind a successful merger of an archetype [that] exists—of the opening day—with an alternative approach to reach the same end. It's an example of how, when we think non-traditionally and cooperate among the various groups, we can increase our success significantly.

Amy Goodman began hosting *Democracy Now!* on Pacifica Radio as a temporary series leading up to the Bill Clinton/Bob Dole presidential race of 1996. The rest, as they say, is public broadcasting history. The program is now broadcast on more than three hundred stations nationwide and is available via the radio, TV, and the Internet.

Interview with Amy Goodman

Goodman's guest list for *Democracy Now!* reads like a who's who of the progressive world. She was interviewed in February 2005 by Evan Derkacz.

DERKACZ: Everyone has a pet theory on why Bush won. What's yours?

GOODMAN: If he won.

DERKACZ: If he won, right.

GOODMAN: Well, we know he didn't win in 2000, and we don't know about now. Because we are increasingly going toward a system that can't be verified, and since in the U.S. elections are held up as the symbol of democracy, it's very important that we be able to verify these elections. The fact that people are suspicious is a very big problem. The fact that you can have places in Ohio where there are 360 voters and 4,200 votes for Bush—this is a big problem. And that's just the places we know. There's also the huge amount of voter suppression and intimidation that goes on for Election Day.

Whether or not he won, even by their count, he [has] something like 30 percent of the [eligible] vote—this isn't very impressive. It is hardly a mandate, and that's what matters, because we have a situation in this country where, for example, most people are opposed to the invasion and occupation of Iraq, and yet the person who is behind that invasion and occupation has won. So I don't think that this is a mandate, certainly [not] for Bush foreign policy.

DERKACZ: Why does the corporate media allow the contours of any debate to be shaped by the Democrats and the Republicans?

GOODMAN: I don't know why. I know that they *do* it. In the book I wrote with my brother, David Goodman, *The Exception to the Rulers*, we talk about the "access of evil"—Bush talks about the "axis of evil"—and that is trading truth for access in order to get the next . . . lie, in order to get the quote from the player himself, whether it's Rumsfeld, Bush, or Cheney. [The media] trade truth for access, and that's unacceptable.

The government needs journalists more than the journalists need the government. The journalists should be standing up and not acting as a megaphone for those in power. I mean, that's not our job. There's a reason why our profession, journalism, is the only one explicitly protected by the U.S. Constitution. Because we are the checks and balances on government, we are supposed to hold those in power accountable, not cozy up to them.

DERKACZ: Why do you think the right-wing echo chamber—from the Heritage Foundation to Fox [News] to Rush Limbaugh—has been so effective in setting the debate?

GOODMAN: They took the media very seriously from the beginning and have built up this right-wing media infrastructure, and it has had an impact. I don't think it's just Fox. It's all the networks. But what cable provided that we didn't have before with the networks was twenty-four hours of news. People are really hungry for information. In a globalized world, people do care about what's happening here and [in] other places in the world.

Now, much of it is rhetoric, much of it is just propaganda, but it's someplace where you're not getting sitcoms, where you're not getting soap operas, where you can actually tap into information about what's happening. So I don't think it's hopeless.

I also think that Bush not finding weapons of mass destruction exposed more than the Bush administration—it exposed the media that acted as a conveyor belt for the lies of the administration. It's not just Fox that was alleging it, it was CNN, it was MSNBC, it was NBC, ABC, it was the *New York Times*, it was the *Washington Post*, day after day, front-page, above-the-fold, lead stories in the newspapers and television about weapons of mass destruction.

Bush could not have done it alone with a little megaphone on the steps of the White House. People would not have believed what he was saying. . . .

So when you have something like that, when you have Dan Rather the night of the invasion, the night the bombs began to fall, saying "Good morning, Baghdad," you have Tom Brokaw saying the night the bombs are falling—you know, March 19, 2003—"We don't want to destroy the infrastructure of Iraq because we're going to own that country in a few days," you have to ask, if we had state[-run] media in the United States how would it be any different?

DERKACZ: Where do we go from here? Where should progressives put their energy now with regard to the media?

GOODMAN: The whole issue of taking back the airwaves is an absolutely critical issue right now. Media activism has proven to be *extremely* successful.

The past year you had Michael Powell, chair of the FCC, trying to push through the largest media consolidation this country has ever seen. You had Michael Powell, right, son of Colin Powell— Colin Powell helps to lead the war in Iraq, [while] his son Michael Powell [is] pushing through media deregulation. His father leads the war in Iraq; his son leads the war on diversity of voices at home. Media monopoly and militarism go hand in hand. That unholy alliance has to be broken. We have to "un-embed" the media because that's what threatens democracy.

We have to build our own media infrastructure, and that's what we're doing at *Democracy Now!*

DERKACZ: *Democracy Now!* has been incredibly successful, but how are you and other progressive media outlets going to pull in people who don't share your point of view?

GOODMAN: I really do think that political labels are breaking down.

That's already happening. I travel across the country, and every-where I go, people across the political spectrum come out. Conservative Republicans, like progressives, care about issues of privacy. Conservatives care about corporate control, about media moguls who are gobbling up the smaller stations, about the "Clear Channeling" of America. This is a threat to everyone.

I don't think it's political labels anymore—that it's so easy to figure out that only one group will listen to one outlet. I find that everything is breaking down—we have to have a new way of looking at the way people look at the world.

DERKACZ: What do you think about the Internet and blogging—what sort of impact will these kinds of new technologies have?
GOODMAN: The more decentralized, the better; the more sources of information, the better. At *Democracy Now!* we always try to give people more access to lots of different forms of information linking to many different sites, because it's in no one's interest just to rely on one source of information. For too long, the networks have monopolized information and really just channeled one kind of propaganda. We've got to break the sound barrier, and we do that by [getting] many people involved, so I support as many ways of getting out any kind of information as possible—it makes us all healthier, it protects us all.

Televangelism
on the Rise

Jeffrey Chester is executive director JEFFREY CHESTER
of the Center for Digital Democracy.

Besides mainstream broadcasters like NBC, Fox, and Sinclair, Democrats and progressives now face a formidable electronic media infrastructure created by Christian churches. Its many outlets produce and distribute "news," commentary, and cultural guides, in a variety of formats. As the British newspaper the *Guardian* recently reported, "If you seriously wanted to take the pulse of America, you had to tune your TV to the news division of televangelism," Pat Robertson's *700 Club*.

Evangelical and Catholic churches played a pivotal role in reelecting President Bush. Through a coordinated effort using its media outlets, the religious right was able to frame the debate and mobilize voter registration. Designed to be below the radar of the news media and Democrats, these GOP religious allies unleashed an arsenal of tactics, including sophisticated Internet organizing.

Now the religious community is preparing to make a serious leap in how it uses its media assets. It is exploring harnessing the power of high-definition television (HDTV), digital radio, streaming broadband, blogs, and RSS feeds.

Religious institutions have long recognized the power of electronic media to advance their interests. They have successfully staked out control over valuable media territory, including radio, TV, cable, and satellite.

Robertson recognized the power of cable early. Though he sold his channel for billions to Rupert Murdoch (who in turn sold it to Disney/ABC), he retained key rights to distribute his daily programs. He and his son also syndicate other shows, including *Christian World News*, the youth-oriented *One-Cubed*, and the magazine-style *Living the Life*.

TV ministries have proven so financially successful that they can now focus on politics and advocacy. Many televangelist programs preached directly against Kerry's candidacy, and gay marriage provided their biggest single issue during the months leading up to the elections. Meanwhile, on *Catholic Live*, host Father Mitch Pacwa stated, "If you vote for a pro-abortion candidate because you agree with him, that's formally sinful."

Religious groups have long worked to access modern communications. The American Family Radio Network has accrued at least 157 stations in a remarkably short period of time. Their success stories include James Dobson's *Focus on the Family*, heard daily on hundreds of stations. Their broadcasts are archived and available online.

But the Christian right's biggest gains are in cable and direct-broadcast satellite. There's Falwell's Liberty Channel, Oral Roberts's Ministries broadcasts, and the Catholic Church's EWTN, on cable in English and Spanish. The Inspiration Channel is also widely available.

Today, these Christian networks are also reaching out via the Web. They have organized the National Religious Broadcasters (www.nrb.org) to advance their interests. This group maintains alliances with the commercial media industry, engaging in political deal making to gain access. In these efforts, it has supported Rupert Murdoch and allied itself with major cable companies to oppose consumer-friendly policies.

Fighting
DAVID Dirty
MORRIS

David Morris is cofounder and vice president of the Institute for Local Self-Reliance in Minneapolis, Minnesota. The following is an excerpt from an article he wrote for AlterNet in December 2004.

One of the reasons liberals lose elections is because liberals approach politics differently from conservatives, at least conservatives circa 2004.

Conservatives view politics as war. In war, one tries to demoralize and destroy the enemy, seize his territory and gain unconditional surrender. Liberals engage in politics as a contact sport. Rule breakers receive penalties, including being thrown out of the game. And when the game ends, people shake hands and differences are set aside.

This difference in approach results in a difference in tactics and strategy. The 2004 Democratic National Convention was a positive affair, pro-Kerry, not anti-Bush. The Republican National Convention was a savage anti-Kerry affair. Contrast Barack Obama's speech with that of Zell Miller and you get the point.

Throughout the campaign, Kerry was reluctant to focus on George W. Bush's absence in the National Guard. Republicans, on the other hand, financed a seven-month, no-holds-barred vicious effort by Swift Boat Veterans for Truth falsely accusing Kerry of being a traitor. The Democratic Party's response? "No fair."

In 1989, Newt Gingrich filed charges against House Speaker Jim Wright (D-Texas) for using bulk purchases of a vanity book to earn excessive speaking fees. But Democrats did not defend Wright, sheepishly maintaining that he did engage in unethical conduct. Wright resigned from office.

Fast-forward to 2004. House Speaker Tom Delay (R-Texas) was censured twice for unethical conduct. The Republican response? They attempted to change the rules to allow him to continue as Speaker, even if indicted!

When John Ashcroft's nomination [for] attorney general came before the Senate, Russell Feingold insisted, "A Republican president ought to be able to appoint people of strong conservative ideology." Can you imagine a Republican senator uttering [a similar sentiment] of a Democratic president's liberal nominee? Remember Lani Guinier?

Conservatives are driven by rage. Liberals are driven by guilt. Conservatives suffer no moral qualms when they engage in dirty tactics. The ends justify the means. Civilization is at stake. Liberals worry that if they do evil they will become evil.

I want liberals running the country. I want people who believe in tolerance and diversity and civility, and yes, even guilt, to hold the reigns of governmental power. But I fear that liberals make a woefully inadequate opposition.

Which leads to the key question: Can we fight fair and win? Or on the flip side, if we adopt conservative tactics, will we lose the very soul of liberalism?

LOOKING FORWARD

THE IRAQ WAR

1

Rethinking Iraq LAKSHMI CHAUDHRY

A month before the 2004 elections, Pulitzer Prize–winning journalist Seymour Hersh predicted the consequences of a George W. Bush victory for Iraq. "If Bush wins reelection, he will bomb and bomb and bomb," he said. "Civilian targets, civilian neighborhoods." He was right.

Within a week of being reelected, the administration launched a no-holds-barred offensive against the Iraqi city of Fallujah. Unlike the first assault in 2003, this time no building was out of bounds in a strategy that was summed up by Capt. Paul Fowler in the *Boston Globe*: "The only way to root them out is to destroy everything in your path." When the first air strike targeted the city's sole hospital, the *New York Times* explained—without comment—the Pentagon's rationale: "The offensive also shut down what officers said was a propaganda weapon for the militants: Fallujah General Hospital, with its stream of reports of civilian casualties."

No one knows how many died in the attack, civilian or otherwise. No one cared to ask—not the mainstream media, not the Democrats, not the American public. Iraq was also absent from the extensive electoral postmortem as pundits, leaders, and opinion makers publicly argued vociferously on every subject—moral values, economics, the Democratic Party leadership, political strategy, race—but the one issue that drove progressive politics in 2004. The unprecedented level of grassroots organizing that characterized John Kerry's campaign would not have been possible without the antiwar movement. The invasion of Iraq in

2003 galvanized progressives of all stripes and brought them out on the streets.

During the primaries, antiwar activists rallied behind Howard Dean, who emerged as the only major presidential candidate to oppose the war. But in the end, "electability" trumped all other issues as the majority of Democrats put aside their antiwar sentiments to vote for John Kerry. Desperate to oust Bush from the White House, few wanted to take the risk of picking an antiwar candidate—not with the memory of George McGovern's ignominious defeat by Richard Nixon still looming large in the party's memory. When Kerry won the party's nomination, progressives rallied around him under the "Anybody But Bush" banner.

The irony was unmistakable. The campaign of a candidate who voted to authorize the invasion of Iraq was being driven by his supporters' opposition to that very same decision. In the following months, however, the Republicans would take each of Kerry's perceived strengths and turn it into a fatal weakness, be it his position on Iraq or his service in Vietnam. They paired his two votes on Iraq—the first to give Bush the power to declare war and the other against an appropriations bill—to paint him as a morally indecisive flip-flopper who couldn't be trusted to lead the country at a time of crisis.

The strategy worked because Kerry's position on Iraq suffered from the same key shortcomings that undermined his larger campaign. He was unable to articulate a clear moral position on one of the most important issues facing the nation and the world. When mocked by Bush for criticizing the very same war that he had authorized, Kerry responded with a complex argument about executive power: Bush as president should have been given the authority to wage war but then bore the responsibility to do so only as a last resort. When that line of reasoning proved ineffective, Kerry fell back on criticizing Bush's competence, including the lack of a postwar plan, his poor diplomatic skills, intelligence failures, and on and on. While the evidence was damning, it lacked the moral resonance to counter the appeal of a presidency that offered certitude in an increasingly dangerous world. A real answer required moral vision—it required Kerry to admit that the war, and therefore his vote to authorize it, was a terrible mistake.

The war is wrong, and most Americans know it. Unlike terrorism or the culture wars, Iraq is the one issue over which progressives have successfully put the Bush administration on the defensive. Our voice has been powerful and compelling, as we've stood stead-fastly for compassion in the face of violence, whether speaking out on behalf of underequipped soldiers or innocent civilians or mal-nourished Iraqi children. Iraq may not have been enough reason for the American public to punish the Republicans in 2004, but all of Karl Rove's machinations—or even the fabled Iraq elections held on January 30, 2005—are not going to make this political time bomb go away. A *Washington Post* poll conducted in December 2004 marked the first time a decisive majority, 56 per-cent, of Americans came to the conclusion that the Iraq war is simply "not worth fighting." More important, a full 70 percent now believe that any gains to U.S. security from Saddam Hussein's departure have come at an "unacceptable" cost in military casual-ties. The survey also identifies a dangerous trend for the adminis-tration: support for the occupation is steadily shrinking to die-hard Republicans, with self-identified independents becoming as skep-tical as Democrats about the current Iraq policy.

So as we face four more years of George Bush, it is our moral opposition to the U.S. occupation that offers the greatest oppor-tunity to build a broad-based movement for change. But in order to succeed, the spontaneous, loose-knit antiwar effort built around marches and symbolic protests has to mature into a tightly organ-ized, disciplined political campaign with a well-honed agenda and plan of action. There are four key goals that everyone committed to ending the war in Iraq must work toward over the coming months: bring the soldiers home; support the creation of a gen-uinely democratic and stable Iraq; hone an effective antiterrorism strategy that reflects a progressive foreign policy agenda; and expand the antiwar movement.

Bringing the Soldiers Home

The occupation has to end. Each day that the United States stays in Iraq brings death and suffering for all involved. The devastation of Iraq is plain to see, even if impossible to measure, thanks to the Pentagon's refusal to count the Iraqi dead. Each day brings news of more civilian casualties, adding to the 100,000 already estimated in October 2004 by a study published in *Lancet*, a British medical journal. No one knows how many more have been disabled, maimed, or traumatized by the U.S. efforts to bring freedom and democracy to Iraq. The price of war on the occupiers, however, is more invisible. The 1,400-plus death toll does not begin to weigh the burdens of war being shouldered by American soldiers. It doesn't count the wounded, who represent a better measure of the price of war at a time when modern medicine is able to save a person's life despite horrific injuries.

The Pentagon counts 10,000 combat-related casualties of war, but there are tens of thousands of *non*-combat-related injuries that are airbrushed out of this carefully edited picture of the occupation. More than 31,000 veterans have sought disability benefits for physical or psychological injuries. And most medical and military experts concede that post-traumatic stress disorder—which can lead to alcoholism, spousal abuse, homelessness, and suicide—will likely affect up to one in three of all returning soldiers.

Yes, the costs of this occupation are indeed unacceptable. But to bring the soldiers home, we need to develop a plan that pushes for the phased departure of U.S. troops rather than hold out for a Vietnam-style dramatic about-face. As Foreign Policy in Focus expert Erik Leaver points out in his five-point plan for a better strategy in Iraq, one of the initiatives should be to reduce troop presence as we shift both law and order and reconstruction duties onto the shoulders of Iraqis.

The other prong of this strategy would be to push for an end to the occupation first—i.e., to transfer the control of Iraq to a truly multinational force. As long as the United States remains in charge, the insurgency will continue to grow, Iraqi security forces will be reluctant to take on the burden of defending an imperial project, and innocent Iraqis will remain trapped in the crossfire of an unjust war. "Who would come?" former general Anthony Zinni asked reporters when pressed on the possibility of international assistance. Well, it's time we made a good-faith effort to raise that question. The world—especially the European and Arab nations— cannot afford a chaotic or unstable Iraq any more than the United States can. An open willingness to cede real power—hardly the hallmark of the Bush policy—may well spark more enthusiasm among our allies.

A Democratic and Stable Iraq

Many antiwar activists support one simple plan for Iraq: bring the troops home. There's been very little discussion of the fallout of such a strategy on the grounds that the very fact of removing the U.S. presence from Iraq would be an improvement per se. In other words, proponents argue, whatever the consequences— for Iraqis, the Middle East, or antiterrorism—the situation could only be better than what we have now. Before long, however, supporters of immediate withdrawal find themselves on difficult moral ground. Bill Maher, for example, is wont to argue that it's presumptuous to assume that Arabs want democracy or freedom.

Others offer a more nuanced argument for withdrawal and believe that that the only moral position is to let Iraqis decide their own fate. As Jonathan Schell argues:

> Let there be as orderly a transition as possible, accompanied by as much aid, foreign assistance and general sweetness and light as can be mustered, but the endpoint, complete withdrawal, should be announced in advance, so that everyone in Iraq—from the beheaders and other murderers, to legitimate resisters, to any true democrats who may be on the scene—can know that the responsibility for their country's future is shifting to their shoulders. The outcome, though not in all honesty likely to be pretty, will

at any rate be the best one possible. If the people of Iraq slip back into dictatorship, it will be their dictatorship. If they choose civil war, it will be their civil war. And if by some happy miracle they choose democracy, it will be their democracy—the only kind worth having.

Underlying each of these arguments—including Schell's—is the assumption that a U.S.-led plan for a viable democracy in Iraq is simply not possible. As a result, we find ourselves advocating for one set of values at home—equality, freedom, and economic security—while jettisoning them in the name of advocating a lesser evil in Iraq. So where Bush talks of Iraqis' rights to a better future—however self-servingly—we speak only of our rights to the same. Bring our soldiers home so that our sons and daughters can be safe; our communities can prosper; our lives will be more secure. These are all sane and reasonable positions, but they lack moral force. We repeatedly take the president to task for lying about his plan to bring freedom and security to Iraq, but we refuse to advocate for policies that would force him to do so.

The other troubling aspect of the get-the-hell-out position is the glaring absence of any sense of moral responsibility. We can't simply turn our backs on the millions of Iraqis who lack basic necessities like water, electricity, food, or medical care just because many of us didn't vote for the man who caused their suffering. Is it moral for us to leave them to die in the crossfire of a violent civil war, fueled by extremists that we created? Chaos creates a political vacuum that is almost always filled by the power-hungry and the ruthless. So what will a Taliban-style regime in Iraq mean for Iraqi women? What effects will it have on the rest of the Middle East, which is already a tinderbox waiting for the careless spark of instability? Will an unstable Iraq really improve hopes for a genuine and just peace in the Middle East? These are not questions that we can afford to shrug off in the heat of antiwar rhetoric. Taken together, they constitute a giant question mark about the connection between our politics and our values.

The first order of business for the antiwar movement, therefore, must be to recover its moral footing by becoming a pro-democracy movement. We must take the president at his word and force him to deliver on the promise of freedom. We were right in claiming that no good could come of invading Iraq. But being right doesn't excuse us from the obligation of doing right by the Iraqi people. We can and should call both for an end to the occupation and for a brighter future for Iraq.

Toward a Progressive Security Policy

The greatest failing of the Kerry campaign was that it never put the war in Iraq—or Bush's decision to wage it—on trial but instead confirmed the dominant wisdom that the antiwar position was simply too far outside the mainstream to merit consideration. Yet simply opposing the war would not have solved the Democratic Party's problems. Kerry's larger weakness was that he never fully articulated an alternative Iraq policy. His arguments were instead based on defending the status quo—a weakness that characterizes traditional liberal politics in general, be it on foreign policy or the economy. It's no accident that Kerry harped ceaselessly on the administration's policy of unilateralism, which he painted as a dangerous break from the central tenets of U.S. foreign policymaking since the Second World War. Other than vague statements about bringing in allies and working with the United Nations, Kerry had little to offer voters except a promise to return to the traditional multilateral approach. His message: let's go back to the old way of doing things. Republicans immediately responded by accusing him of having a pre-9/11 mentality. It was an especially damaging accusation at a time when 75 percent of Bush supporters in October still believed that Saddam Hussein was connected in one way or another to al Qaeda.

Kerry's problems reflect a deeper weakness in the antiwar movement. In a post-9/11 era, opposition to a war—however immoral or dangerous—will never gain wide support unless it also addresses the American public's genuine fears of terrorism. The Bush "war on terror" offers a simple strategy: take the fight to the enemy by whatever means necessary. It's an approach that ensures blanket support for almost any measure the administration might choose to take in the name of this war, be it invading Iraq or rounding up immigrants without a trial. As a result, even though many Bush voters no longer supported the occupation of Iraq, they still voted for the president. People who are scared will not abandon a leader who is doing *something* to fight terrorism just because it's not working. Americans needed to hear a clear, well-thought-out alternative plan to keep them safe. Neither Kerry nor the antiwar movement gave them that choice.

This void offers the perfect window of opportunity for so-called liberal hawks eager to jump on the "war on terror" bandwagon. In December, the editor of the *New Republic*, Peter Beinart, created a stir with an article titled "A Fighting Faith," which accused liberals of ignoring the peril of "totalitarian Islam" in a post-9/11 world. The only way forward, Beinart argued, is to create a more muscular, hawkish version of liberalism, which would embrace the use of force, push for development-oriented economic aid, and most important, purge the liberal movement of anyone who dissents—namely Michael Moore and MoveOn. The essay was as equally cavalier in its use of the word *totalitarian* to describe all Islam as it was in painting progressives as lily-livered "softs."

For the most part, Beinart was less interested in making "an argument for a new liberalism" than in using Kerry's defeat to lobby for a brand of hawkish Democratic politics that had been with us long before John F. Kennedy blundered into the Bay of Pigs. Yet it's an argument that requires a response if the antiwar movement is to be taken seriously. The most significant obstacle in building an effective opposition to the war is the perception that all progressives are "soft" on terrorism. In other words, we're not interested in battling any foe, period—be it Saddam or al Qaeda. The charge is, of course, unfair and untrue. "The dynamic is simple—we've been in the opposition and on defense," MoveOn founder Wes Boyd told *Salon*. "So when the president says that the way to fight terrorism is to fight a war in Iraq, the opposition says, 'Wait a second, are you insane?' That's perceived as not caring about terrorism." Boyd, however, thinks it's now time to go on the offensive with "the development of a security policy that is strong and hard."

The threat of terrorism is real. It poses a threat to innocent people around the world, whether in a building in Manhattan, in a nightclub in Bali, on a school bus in Tel Aviv, in the mountains of Kashmir, or on the streets of Baghdad. We must be as fierce in our opposition to extremism abroad as we are at home. So far we have been content to critique the policies of the Bush administration, offering only a few scattered suggestions in response. But a proposal to check commercial cargo on an airplane or to strengthen the ports just seems like more "gotcha" politics in the absence of a coherent security policy. And given our sensitivity to the complex realities of global politics, progressives, in fact, are better suited to craft an effective, pragmatic strategy than the chest-thumping hawks on either side of the aisle.

For all the energy and resources progressives have invested in specific international issues over the years—Vietnam, Iran-Contra, and now Iraq—we have never developed a coherent foreign policy vision. We have been defined instead by our dissent. When the Soviet Union fell, the neoconservatives saw it as an opportunity for a far-reaching, aggressive vision of U.S. military power. Progressives instead got busy pushing for cuts in Pentagon spending or moved on to protesting globalization. It's time for us to think big and think positive.

The Antiwar Movement of Tomorrow

Iraq is still the linchpin of the progressive movement. It has the potential to become the galvanizing issue of a broad-based, reenergized grassroots effort that reaches far beyond our traditional allies. As the Bush administration continues to pursue its failing strategy in Iraq, there is no doubt that the war will grow steadily more unsustainable. The months to come will offer valuable opportunities to reach out to soldiers and their families who are becoming rapidly disenchanted with an occupation that is wearing them thin. Veterans groups will grow more vocal, as will moderate Republicans who are no longer ready to remain silent in the name of party unity, giving us the opportunity to grow stronger and more powerful than ever before.

Our most valuable and credible allies in the fight to end the occupation will be the soldiers themselves. There are already signs of growing unrest among the soldiers, a number of whom are in open rebellion. From Donald Rumsfeld's embarrassing run-in with disgruntled National Guardsmen in Baghdad—who openly challenged the defense secretary over their lack of proper equipment—to the desertion of soldiers like Jeremy Hinzman to Canada, the Pentagon is having a difficult time hiding the plummeting morale among the rank and file. Adding to the sense of alienation are the Department of Defense's "stop loss" orders that force soldiers to stay on active duty even after their contract has expired. The indisputable evidence of this loss of faith in the Pentagon is a recent army survey that shows that half the active-duty soldiers in Iraq were not planning to reenlist.

The futility and horror of this unjust war are turning many Iraqi war veterans into passionate antiwar advocates. Rob Sarra—a nine-year Marine veteran who once saw antiwar protesters as "hippies" who hated the military—became the cofounder of Iraq Veterans Against the War after he came home from the front. He now speaks out at any opportunity he gets—on college campuses, in protest marches, in high schools.

Growing a movement, however, is not just about numbers. Unless antiwar activists begin connecting the war to broader issues such as freedom, economic opportunity, and patriotism, our voices will never be heard by the vast number of Americans for whom the violence is just another gruesome image on television. If we stick to single-issue politics as usual, the outcome is also going to remain unchanged. The war represents a historic moment that can do more than just reenergize the antiwar constituency; it can also kick-start a powerful movement to transform all aspects of America. This is why our strategy must reflect and inform our broader moral and political vision, whose principles apply equally at home and abroad.

The task is indeed a difficult one. There are significant trade-offs between the goals outlined here, and tensions that we need to acknowledge and address. For example, can we bring our soldiers home *and* fulfill our responsibility toward the Iraqi people? Will talk of reparations limit the efforts to broaden the antiwar movement? There are no simple answers to these questions, which test our moral judgment and priorities. Even Boyd admits to being torn: "Our membership is split on immediate withdrawal versus the sense that if you break it, it's yours to take care of. I feel that same split myself."

Perhaps we all could do well to learn from some of the very soldiers we want to bring home. An Army reserve specialist who suffered a spine-shattering injury in Iraq, Denver Jones speaks not of his own suffering but that of the Iraqis: "Just because someone is in a 'Third World' country, they're not different than I am. They're human beings and . . . God's children. Because I have been blessed with the opportunity to achieve what I have, it doesn't mean that as a human being . . . I'm more deserving or any better than they are." Though the 35-year-old former UPS mechanic would likely never call himself one, he represents the very best of the values of progressives. Let's not ask any less of ourselves.

Best known for her brilliant analysis of corporate marketing in *No Logo: Taking Aim at the Brand Bullies,* Naomi Klein has long been a voice for moral accountability in the media. Since 2003, the 34-year-old Canadian has found a new calling: speaking out against the war in Iraq. In her internationally syndicated column—which appears in

Interview with Naomi Klein

the *Globe and Mail* in Canada and the *Guardian* in Britain—Klein exposes the sadly undercovered economic colonization of Iraq in the name of "reconstruction," which is no less brutal or devastating than the Pentagon-led destruction of the countryside. She was interviewed in January 2005 by Lakshmi Chaudhry.

CHAUDHRY: You've taken on the John Kerry campaign for its failure to tackle Iraq. How did that play to the GOP's advantage?

KLEIN: Karl Rove understood that if he wanted to galvanize his base, he should make sure they could vote for the things that stirred the strongest passions—which in his analysis were abortion and gay marriage. The Kerry campaign took the exact opposite approach. They felt that the best strategy was to muzzle their base on the issue that they cared [about] most passionately: the war in Iraq. And the campaign so took for granted their loyalty that they ran a pro-war campaign.

Another part of the failure has to do with the way you answer the language of faith. You don't answer the language of faith with the language of more effective bureaucracy, which is the image that John Kerry's campaign presented: more effective administrators, more effective bureaucrats of war. You have to answer the language of faith with the language of morality. You can speak in powerful moral terms about the violence of war and the violence of an economic system that's excluding ever more people.

That didn't happen because there were no policies in the Kerry campaign that coincided with that language of morality. These were policies such as a withdrawal from Iraq, an end to the violence, and serious economic alternatives at home, which weren't on the table either. The campaign, in essence, tinkered with the Bush agenda, along with [delivering] a message that they were more credible than Bush.

CHAUDHRY: When you talk about moral language, it's remarkable that Kerry didn't once mention Abu Ghraib.

KLEIN: I think there was a lot of disdain in the Kerry campaign. The disdain that bothered me more was the disdain that they showed for the Iraqi people in their total unwillingness to condemn the basic violations of human rights and international law. [Kerry] didn't mention Abu Ghraib. He didn't ever mention civilian deaths as one of the problems in Iraq. He was too busy showing how tough he was. [The campaign] clearly made a decision that speaking about Abu Ghraib and Guantánamo would seem to be critical of the troops. And to speak about Iraqi civilians and international law would be to appear soft on the war on terror.

Once you accept these premises—which are premises that were laid out by the Bush administration—you're playing on their turf. You don't win on their turf; you win by redefining it. I believe that Kerry's campaign was utterly morally bankrupt, and I blame the Kerry campaign for the total impunity that the Bush administration is now enjoying.

First of all, I believe that an antiwar campaign could have won the election. But even if you think I'm crazy, I believe that an antiwar campaign would have done a better job at losing the election [*laughs*]. An election campaign was the one time there was a real opportunity to put the war on trial. And even if a principled antiwar campaign had lost, these issues would still be on the agenda.

CHAUDHRY: So where does the antiwar movement go from here? What kind of rethinking is necessary now?

KLEIN: The great error made during the electoral campaign was that the antiwar movement allowed itself to turn into an anti-Bush movement. So as the logic of anyone-but-Bush set in—and there wasn't a candidate speaking on these issues—the war itself disappeared. What I mean by that is that the *reality of war* itself disappeared. The truth is that we were talking about Iraq in the past tense, not about what was happening on the ground during the campaign. And indeed, I believe that continues to be true to a scandalous degree, especially [considering] what we've just seen in recent months in Iraq. I'm worried that we haven't learned from that mistake yet.

We also need to focus more clearly on policy demands. I have been arguing for a long time that the antiwar movement should turn itself into a pro-democracy movement, i.e., support the demands for democracy in Iraq. There are clear demands that are coming out of Iraq. And if we care to listen, we can mirror them and bring them home to where the decisions are being made in Washington, in London, and so on. We haven't done much of that.

What we've really done a lot of is proving ourselves right to have even opposed the war in the first place. And I even sometimes get the sense—in some antiwar circles—that we who oppose the war don't have any responsibility to talk about how to improve the situation in Iraq beyond just advocating pulling out the troops.

I have heard people on the left in the United States say that we don't owe Iraq anything, that they have oil revenue, that our only responsibility is to just pull out. That is wrong. Our responsibility goes far beyond that. Anybody who says that has really not taken a hard look at the level of devastation of that country.

CHAUDHRY: What's a specific policy or issue that the antiwar movement could rally around?

KLEIN: For me the easiest issue is debt. The Iraqis should not have to inherit Saddam's debt. This is a very simple issue. Now this is something Bush has said and James Baker has said. And that's why we feel we don't have the right to say it. The truth is that when Bush and Baker say it, they're lying. What they've actually done to Iraq instead is reduce the debt just enough to make sure that Iraqis can repay it. It was at a completely unsustainable level and was never going to be repaid previously so it was restructured—so that they could demand that it be repaid. Then it was attached to an IMF structural adjustment program that makes debt forgiveness contingent on adherence to incredibly damaging and dangerous new economic [free market] policies.

We said nothing about this in the antiwar movement when we should have been demanding total debt erasure. We had a window when Bush was using our language, but instead we responded as if we didn't have any responsibility to do so *because* he was using that language.

We need to develop an agenda based on the demands coming from Iraq for reparations, for total debt erasure, for complete control over the oil revenues, for a cancellation of the contracts signed under the occupation, and so on. This is what real sovereignty would look like, real self-determination—we know this.

CHAUDHRY: You've been to Iraq—how do Iraqis view this demand for immediate withdrawal?
KLEIN: The country is so wrecked. In the absence of any other source of hope, there are people in Iraq who worry that the troop withdrawal would just signify a complete abandonment of country.

Quite frankly, there's a lot of skepticism in Iraq—from what I saw—about the international antiwar movement. In part, it's because antiwar forces were not critical enough of Saddam. But it's also because we haven't proposed this kind of practical solidarity that has to do with improving people's lives, and not just absolving our conscience. Or saying "Not in our name," and then going home.

CHAUDHRY: One of the criticisms against the antiwar movement is also that we haven't put forward policy alternatives. Do you agree?
KLEIN: It's very, very frustrating. What I keep coming across in the U.S. antiwar movement is the acceptance of this idea that Americans are incapable of caring about anyone but themselves. The progressives in the United States are fairly self-loathing in that

basically we allow ourselves to oppose a specific policy, but we completely internalize the values and the principles of the right—ideas such as Americans can only care about selfish demands; they can't really care about people in another country; to talk about international law in the United States is to be seen as giving up U.S. power to foreigners.

We basically accept all of this instead of making passionate arguments in favor of international law that would actually convince people. In a lot of cases, the policies are there but we don't have the strength of our convictions to make them. We buy far too easily into the belief that these are too far outside the mainstream, too far outside the box, and Americans will never go for it. So we're too cowardly to put forward real policy alternatives and we only allow ourselves to critique, and therefore [we] become not credible.

CHAUDHRY: So what are the immediate tasks facing the antiwar movement right now?

KLEIN: The first task is to develop a positive agenda with progressive forces in Iraq—to support deep democracy and genuine sovereignty in that country, which would make the demand for troop withdrawal credible.

The second goal is to have an international strategy to increase the pressure on the U.S. military so that continued U.S. presence becomes increasingly untenable. That means trying to further break the coalition and identifying points of vulnerability. The coalition is very vulnerable—particularly in countries like Italy, Japan, and even the UK, where a majority of the population is clearly against the war. Increasing the pressure there for withdrawal then increases the burden on U.S. troops and makes the demand for troop withdrawal stronger. In Canada I think we have a role to play by supporting the war deserters who have come here, particularly the push for a legal precedent to be set for American soldiers claiming refugee status in Canada. If we win a couple of these legal cases, there will be many more American soldiers who will want to come. The goal should be to get the Bush administration to the point where they have to choose between staying in Iraq and bringing in the draft.

CHAUDHRY: Isn't that a little hazardous from a political point of view, in the sense that you could be seen as advocating against the soldiers or pushing for a draft?

KLEIN: Everything I'm saying is slightly politically hazardous. But I'm talking about the global antiwar movement now. There are certain demands more important to be made in the United States, and then there has to be a strategy for the rest of the world. And the strategy for the rest of the world should be to send a clear message to the Bush administration: if you truly want to be the unilateral administration, then you must bear the burden of your unilateralism.

The Reality of War

In the fall of 2004, AlterNet talked to soldiers, as well as a neurosurgeon who had treated wounded soldiers, in an effort to document the horrors of the Iraq war. While there has been considerable coverage of the official version of the war, not enough attention has been paid to the Americans who served—and experienced—the reality of the war. The following are excerpts from interviews conducted by Lakshmi Chaudhry.

Afghanistan and Iraq War Veteran Gene Bolles

Gene Bolles, a 62-year-old neurosurgeon, answered a call from the Department of Defense after 9/11 and spent about two years as the chief neurosurgeon at the Landstuhl Regional Medical Center, the U.S. military hospital in Germany that receives all injured soldiers evacuated from Iraq and Afghanistan.

CHAUDHRY: What kind of cases did you treat in Landstuhl? And these were mostly kids, right?

BOLLES: They were 18, 19, maybe 21. They all seemed very young. Certainly younger than my children. As a neurosurgeon I mostly dealt with injuries to the brain, the spinal cord, or the spine itself. The injuries were all fairly horrific, anywhere from loss of extremities, multiple extremities, to severe burns. It just goes on and on and on. There were just a lot of serious injuries. As a doctor myself who has seen trauma throughout his career—I've never seen it to this degree. The numbers, the degree of injuries—it really kinda caught me off guard.

CHAUDHRY: What about the soldiers themselves?

BOLLES: The soldiers, initially because of how they're trained, don't think of themselves. They're thinking of the buddies they've left behind. Almost all of them don't accept the reality of what's happened to them. They're still back in the war zone. And they care about their buddies so much.

And this is what makes the soldiers do what they do so gallantly—this feeling for each other. So when they get injured, they first feel guilty that they're not still back with their buddies. But then as time goes on, they realize the price they paid for the war and then there is anger. And then there is frustration, then sadness, then depression. They realize they may never walk again or are so disfigured that the rest of their life is going to be very difficult.

But when they're going through this depression, we don't write about them so much. We don't display them. We want to . . . look at [only] those soldiers who have . . . recovered from it or those who are acting as though nothing has happened. It's because we want to look at them as heroes. And they *are* heroes. But it's a reality that is not talked about much.

CHAUDHRY: Many experts predict that post-traumatic stress disorder is going to be to the Iraq war what Agent Orange was to the Vietnam War. Do you agree?

BOLLES: Yes. I have talked to many people who've been in the war zone. Many would break down talking about seeing their buddy get hurt or killed. They would even talk about the Iraqi soldiers— how awful it was, all that carnage. One guy hadn't slept for a long time because of nightmares because of what he saw early in the war, when we were killing high numbers of Iraqis. And he saw some of them get run over by tanks. He just couldn't get those images out of his mind. They talk about hearing screams of comrades or enemies or civilians or children. To see it and be there creates a lot of reaction. Sometimes they might initially act really tough, but underneath it all most soldiers have a lot of humane feeling. They feel this horror very deeply, more than many are willing to admit.

CHAUDHRY: According to some of the veterans groups, 33,000 soldiers have sought VA care; 26,000 have filed VA disability claims; and 10,000 have sought VA counseling. When you look at these huge numbers, what do they indicate?

BOLLES: It's just starting, and it's only going to get worse. Those numbers are going to do nothing but increase. You have the physical injuries, which speak for themselves. I've seen the breakdown of that 33,000 number [soldiers who have sought VA care], and they include a significant percent of spine injuries. These are people in a lot of chronic pain. They're seeking help from our VA system, which is undergoing changes and is still underfunded. So these people don't get the help they really need. There's a lot of people suffering from post-traumatic stress syndrome, [and] that number is going to go up and up and up as time goes on.

CHAUDHRY: How have these very emotional years affected you?
BOLLES: I think about it a lot when I go to bed at night. I can't get it out of my head. It haunted me then and it haunts me now—the horrific, horrific injuries that these young people will now have to deal with for the rest of their lives. And I don't know if I'll ever stop thinking about them. I just feel a tremendous sadness, and that's just the way it is. I just hope everything in the world can be done to make what they have left for the rest of their lives as positive as possible. I sometimes fear that once they come back with all the injuries and damage, they'll be forgotten about very quickly.

Iraq War Veteran
Sean Huze

The day after 9/11/2001, Sean Huze, an actor in Los Angeles, walked into a recruiter's office and enlisted in the U.S. Marine Corps. Sixteen months later, he was sent to Iraq as part of the Second Light Armored Reconnaissance Battalion, leaving behind a wife and young son. Months after his return, he found himself slipping into despair and ended up writing a play called *The Sandstorm*, which the *L.A. Times* praised for "its shocking force and awesome honesty."

I can never be the man I was before I left for Iraq. I had a lot of faith. I was a true believer in the administration's justification for the war—about the weapons of mass destruction and Iraq being an imminent threat. I believed in what we were doing when we were

over there. That belief I had in the administration allowed me to
balance what I was seeing, what I was experiencing, what I was a
part of. With all that death and destruction—the deaths of soldiers and Iraqi civilians who were caught in the crossfire—it
helped that I believed that it was all for a greater good.

Coming home, at first it was about being back with my family—
y'know, the yellow ribbon around the tree, the flags, and the
"Welcome Home" signs. For a few months, I couldn't allow myself
to believe that it was all for a lie.

I know the real transition in me happened when my eyes were
opened—when I realized that there were no weapons of mass
destruction. I realized that Saddam Hussein was not a threat to not
just the United States but to any of the countries on his borders.
That there was no tie to September 11. And these were what I now
believe were intentional misrepresentations and manipulation.

When you realize this, then you don't have anything to balance
everything you've seen and been through. You're just stuck with it.
And it hurts. You have to deal with what you've already been
through—the death and destruction that's haunting you. But now
you're also dealing with a sense of betrayal [of what] you'd trusted
most. That's what I was left with—what I'm still left with.

Iraq War Veteran
Rob Sarra

Rob Sarra went to Iraq as a staff sergeant in the Marine
Corps in January 2003. What he experienced in Iraq—especially the
death of an Iraqi woman—changed him in a profound way. Before he
went to Iraq, he considered antiwar protesters "hippies" who hated the
military; when he returned, he formed the Iraq Veterans Against the War
organization. Here he describes the incident that was the turning point.

I was sitting on top of an armored vehicle about 200 yards away.
A woman starts walking out of this town toward a second armored
vehicle with a bunch of Marines on it. They were waving their
arms and telling her to stop, but she kept moving toward them.
She was dressed in all black, completely covered, wearing a burka.
And she had a bag under one arm.

My thought process at the time was that either she was going to walk up to this vehicle and explode and kill a bunch of Marines or I can take a shot at her and stop it from happening. We'd had reports of suicide bombers in the area. So I raised my rifle and fired two shots. As the second shot went off, the Marines in the other vehicle opened up on her, with everything from M16s to 40-millimeter grenades.

But as she hit the ground, she pulled a white flag out of her bag.

At that point, I was just devastated. I threw my weapon down on the deck of the vehicle and started crying. I just couldn't understand why she hadn't stopped or why it had happened.

That just stayed with me. I think it changed the course of the war for me.

Iraq War Veteran
David Grimm

A former Marine, David Grimm joined the Florida National Guard and went to Iraq in December 2002. Once there, he realized there were separate rules for the reservists and the soldiers on active duty. Before long, the 32-year-old and his fellow guardsmen were writing home, asking for essential equipment that the Pentagon simply refused to provide for reservists.

We got our call-up orders on December 26, 2002. When we went to our mobilization site in Georgia—and as we were being issued all the equipment we were supposed to take—they refused to issue us body armor.

The military was told that since we were National Guard, we weren't going to get body armor. It was our state's responsibility to send us with body armor. The state of Florida said, "No, you're now on federal active duty. It's the federal government's job to supply you with body armor."

We went to Kuwait in April. We were there for almost a month. All the other units at the camp had body armor. We didn't get body armor until after we were in Baghdad for two months. And it took two soldiers being shot before we got body armor. Soldiers were writing home to their parents and begging them to send body armor.

To put it in perspective, when we left Iraq to come back to the United States, before we flew out of Iraq, we had to turn in our body armor so they could ship it back down to Kuwait. There wasn't enough body armor for the soldiers coming in.

How to End the Iraq War

Tom Hayden, a leader of the peace and civil rights movements of the 1960s, served eighteen years in the California legislature, teaches at

TOM HAYDEN

Occidental College in Los Angeles, and is national cochair of No More Sweatshops. The following is excerpted from an article he published on AlterNet shortly after the 2004 elections.

Instead of assuming that the Bush administration has an "exit strategy," the antiwar movement needs to force our government to exit. The strategy must be to deny the U.S. occupation funding, political standing, sufficient troops, and alliances necessary to [its] strategy for dominance.

The first step is to build pressure at congressional district levels to oppose any further funding or additional troops for war. If members of Congress balk at cutting off all assistance and want to propose "conditions" for further aid, it is a small step toward threatening funding. If only seventy-five members of Congress go on record against any further funding, that's a step in the right direction—toward the exit.

The important thing is for antiwar activists to become more grounded in the everyday political life of their districts, organizing antiwar coalitions including clergy, labor, and inner-city representatives to knock loudly on congressional doors and demand that the $200 billion squandered on Iraq go to infrastructure and schools at home. When trapped between imperial elites and their own insistent constituents, members of Congress will tend to side with their voters. That is how the wars in Vietnam and Cambodia were ended in 1975.

Two, we need to build a progressive Democratic movement [that] will pressure the Democrats to become an antiwar opposition party. The antiwar movement has done enough for the Democratic Party this year. It is time for the Democratic leadership to end its collaboration with the Bush administration—with its endorsement of the offensive on Fallujah, the talk of "victory" and "killing the terrorists"—and now play the role of the opposition. The progressive activists of the party should refuse to contribute any more resources—volunteers, money, et cetera—to candidates or incumbents who act as collaborators.

Thought should be given to selectively challenging hawkish Democratic incumbents in primaries and supporting peace candidacies in 2006 and 2008.

Three, we need to build alliances with Republican antiwar conservatives. Nonpartisan antiwar groups (such as Win Without War) should reach out to conservatives who, according to the *New York Times*, are "ready to rumble" against Iraq. Pillars of the American right, including Paul Weyrich, Pat Buchanan, and William F. Buckley, are seriously questioning the quagmire created by the neoconservatives. Strategists like Grover Norquist call the war "a drag on votes" and "threatening to the Bush coalition" that cost Bush six percentage points in the election. The left cannot create a left majority, but it can foster a left-right majority that threatens the hawks in both parties.

Four, we must build solidarity with dissenting combat veterans, reservists, their families, and those who suffered in 9/11. Just as wars cannot be fought without taxpayer funding, wars cannot be fought without soldiers willing to die, even for a mistake. Every person who cares about peace should start their daily e-mail messages with the current body count, including a question mark after the category "Iraqi civilians."

Groups like Iraq Veterans Against the War deserve all the support the rest of the peace movement can give. This approach opens the door to much-needed organizing in both the so-called red states and inner cities, which give disproportionate levels of the lives lost in Iraq.

The movement will need to start opening another underground railroad to havens in Canada for those who refuse to serve, but for now even the most moderate grievances should be supported—for example, relief from the "back-door draft" that is created by extending tours of duty.

Over one-third of some 3,900 combat veterans have resisted their call-ups, and the Army National Guard is at 10 percent of its recruitment goal. More generally, the "superpower" is stretched to a breaking point, with fourteen of the Army's thirty-three combat brigades on front-line duty in Iraq. Though most discourse on Vietnam ignores or underplays the factor of dissent within the American armed forces, it was absolutely pivotal to bringing the ground war to an end. It already is becoming a real "gallstone" for the Pentagon again.

Five, we need to defeat the U.S. strategy of "Iraqization." "Clearly, it's better for us if they're in the front line," Paul Wolfowitz explained last February. This cynical strategy is based on putting an Iraqi "face" on the U.S. occupation in order to reduce the number of American casualties, neutralize opposition in other Arab countries, and slowly legitimize the puppet regime. In truth, it means changing the color of the body count.

The problem for the White House is that if the Iraqi police and troops will not suppress and kill other Iraqis on behalf of the United States, the war effort will completely disintegrate. In April, the 200,000-strong Iraqi security forces assigned to Fallujah simply collapsed. In the most recent battle of Fallujah, the Iraqi troops took part in little if any combat. In Mosul, insurgents seized five Iraqi police stations, not an uncommon event.

There is no sign, aside from Pentagon spin, that an Iraqi force can replace the American occupation in the foreseeable future. Pressure for funding cuts and for an early American troop withdrawal will expose the emptiness of the promise of Iraqization. In Vietnam, the end quickly came when South Vietnamese troops were expected to defend their country. The same is likely to occur in Iraq—or the United States can deepen its dilemma through permanent occupation.

Six, we should work to dismantle the U.S. war "coalition" by building a "Peace Coalition" by the means of the global antiwar movement. Groups with international links (such as Global Exchange or other solidarity groups) could organize conferences and exchanges aimed at uniting public opinion against any regimes with troops supporting the United States in Iraq. Every time an American official shows up in Europe demanding support, there should be speakers from the American antiwar movement offering a rebuttal to the official line.

With U.N. Secretary-General Kofi Annan suggesting that the Iraq policy is illegal, the Bush administration faces the danger of being frozen out of international diplomacy. At some point, the administration will painfully find that it cannot impose its will on everyone on the planet.

In short: pinch the funding arteries, push the Democrats to become an opposition party, ally with antiwar Republicans, support dissenting soldiers, make Iraqization more difficult, and build a peace coalition against the war coalition. If the politicians are too frightened or ideologically incapable of implementing an exit strategy, the only alternative is for the people to pull the plug.

THE CULTURE WAR

2 —————————————

The Return of the Culture War LAKSHMI CHAUDHRY

November 3, 2004, marked not just John Kerry's defeat but also the return of an almost-forgotten phrase to the political lexicon. The "culture wars" were back—and with a vengeance. Within hours of the outcome, pundits were putting forward what would rapidly become the conventional wisdom among the chatterati: uppity amoral liberals got their comeuppance for ignoring the traditional values of regular folk. Where the talk before the election had been dominated by terrorism and Iraq, the day after it was all about God—a punitive God, that is, who hates above all homosexuality and abortion.

The dominant theory about George W. Bush's victory was influenced by exaggerated evaluations of the responses to a single question in the exit polls conducted by the National Election Pool—the same polls that predicted a Kerry victory. Asked to name the one issue that most influenced their choice of candidate, 22 percent of voters picked "moral values" out of a list of seven issues, while "economy/jobs" came in second at 20 percent. Oddly, "Iraq" (15 percent) and "terrorism" (19 percent) were listed separately.

While the exit polls were just a flimsy excuse for the media to indulge in its usual habit of inventing novelty where none exists, the elections did offer a harsh lesson in the power of the religious right. They got their parishioners out in droves to vote their moral opposition to abortion and homosexuality even if it meant supporting a party whose economic policies threatened their livelihood.

No wonder then that the Christian right now sees itself as the architect of Bush's victory. Within days, television screens were plastered with the likes of Jerry Falwell and Gary Bauer, each declaring the triumph of cultural conservatism. In their minds, the evangelicals have now earned their right to sit at the head of the table. As far as they are concerned, it's finally time for the Republican Party to deliver on its hard-right agenda: overthrow *Roe v. Wade*, legalize school prayer, crack down on gay rights, and censor sexual content, whether on the TV screen or in the classroom.

So the right wing thinks it has won the culture war. But has it?

The conventional wisdom on the morals divide is at best simplistic. Bush, for example, made significant gains among pro-choice married women. The same exit polls cited by the media reveal that only 16 percent of voters oppose abortion in all circumstances, and 22 percent of them voted for John Kerry. As for homosexuality, a healthy majority of Americans (63 percent) support either marriage or civil unions. If Bush voters are not all Bible-thumpers, Democrats are hardly secular atheists. They include vast numbers of devoutly religious Americans—Catholics, Muslims, Jews, and yes, even evangelicals, not to mention the nonreligious liberals who voted their moral opposition to the Bush administration's policies, whether on Iraq or the environment.

The disagreement between social conservatives and liberals is not over religion but over the constitutional separation of church and state. A Catholic Democrat may be equally opposed to abortion and any attempt to legislate what is essentially a personal decision. The assumption that all religious Americans support the Christian right agenda is clearly false, as is the conflation of someone who may be uncomfortable with the sight of Janet Jackson's breast on national television with a Jerry Falwell follower.

The 2004 election did not spell the triumph of Christian fundamentalism over godless liberals. It did, however, deliver a damning indictment of a political strategy crippled by the absence of a compelling moral vision. The failure is not just that of the Democratic Party leadership—though it bears a significant share of the blame—but also of the progressive movement as a whole. We have steadfastly refused to acknowledge the power of beliefs, assuming instead that the facts would set all Americans free. We have fallen victim to a culture of oppositional politics, content to vociferously challenge the Republicans without doing the hard work of crafting and communicating a persuasive worldview of our own—a values-based vision of America and the future.

The Not-Republican Party

The notion that white working-class men—better known during the 2004 campaign as the NASCAR dads—are increasingly voting against their interests is hardly news. Both Norman Mailer and Arlie Hochschild have written extensively on the post-9/11 dynamic that led blue-collar men to deeply identify with George Bush's brand of swaggering machismo. Feeling increasingly emasculated by economic insecurity, which threatened not just their income but also their self-image as family providers, blue-collar men sought refuge in the false sense of empowerment offered by a president ever eager to assure them that as Americans, they were both right and mighty.

Their flight into GOP arms, however, was not a fallout of 9/11 but part of an ongoing transformation of the larger political landscape that began in the 1970s. As Thomas Frank argued persuasively in his book *What's the Matter with Kansas?*, the Democratic Party has for decades refused to accept the reality of what he describes as "conservative backlash politics." What began as a response to the counterculture movement of the 1960s has hardened into an ingrained distrust of liberals under the careful guidance of the Republican Party, the well-funded right-wing think tanks, and lately, Fox News and its ilk. Over the past thirty years, the conservative movement has focused its energy and resources on diverting increasing anger over economic hardship toward divisive social wedge issues, such as homosexuality and abortion.

In the post-Reagan era, increasing economic inequality would become an advantage for the GOP. Not only did economic hardship fuel social resentment—against the lazy poor, the job-stealing immigrants, the debauched Hollywood moguls—but it also created a window of opportunity for the Christian right. Writing in *The Nation*, Barbara Ehrenreich brilliantly dissected the insidious relationship between the GOP assault on welfare and the growing influence of right-wing churches, which now offer their parishioners the very same array of public services—free meals, jobs and drugs counseling, child care, et cetera—but with religious strings attached. In her words, these churches "have become an alternative welfare state, whose support rests not only on 'faith' but also on the loyalty of the grateful recipients." It's the kind of loyalty that paid off at the voting booth on Election Day.

The Democratic Party's strategy of moving to the right on the economy has clearly worked against its own interests. Yet it's not surprising that many of the party leaders have responded to the latest electoral debacle with calls to do the same on social issues. Within weeks of the election, the Senate Democrats had selected a pro-life Harry Reid as their leader, even as California Senator Dianne Feinstein blamed San Francisco mayor Gavin Newsom's decision to legalize gay marriages for the party's defeat. No policy or position is indispensable in a party that substitutes strategy for vision.

In his book *Don't Think of an Elephant!*, George Lakoff points out, "People do not necessarily vote in their self-interest. They vote their identity. They vote their values." Yet with the exception of Bill Clinton's first campaign for the presidency in 1992 (which put forward—and then betrayed—the vision for a reenergized liberal politics), the Democratic Party plank has often resembled a grab bag of policies, each carefully tailored not to alienate so-called swing voters while appeasing the array of interest groups that represent core constituencies.

To win, the Democrats must articulate a coherent, persuasive worldview that voters can identify with. The party instead has been content to cede ideological ground to the Republicans with each defeat, and thereby sow the seeds of its own irrelevance.

Soon its leaders will have nothing to offer voters except the promise to be better, more effective Republicans.

The Moral of the Story

Easy as it is to blame the Democratic leadership—and as much as it might deserve the blame—the errors of the party mirror deeper flaws in progressive thinking. After all, it is no accident that someone like Kerry gained the party nomination. In an email to *Tikkun* subscribers, Rabbi Michael Lerner laid bare the perverse logic of the predominantly antiwar Democrats nominating a pro-war candidate: "Privately, they told themselves and each other the following: Kerry is really not for this war. Once he is elected he will, we hope, feel less pressure to be opportunistic, and then the real John Kerry will re-emerge and save us from this war."

So would nominating an antiwar candidate such as Howard Dean have won Democrats the election? Maybe not. The issue here is not one of any specific policy positions but of the absence of moral vision. But there was no consensus—or much thinking, for that matter—on the left as to what a moral Iraq policy might look like in the face of postwar realities. So it's no wonder that we were content to allow Kerry to sell himself on Bush's failings—the lies, the lack of postwar planning, the towering costs—rather than articulate a counter-morality of his own.

After enduring years of relentless political GOP assaults on the progressive ideals, we've all succumbed to the politics of opposition. It has become easier to define ourselves in the negative, by what we stand against rather than what we stand for. And this void constitutes the essence of the right's ideological victory.

The progressives' reluctance to talk moral values springs partly from a self-defeating hubris, which became painfully apparent in debates over religion in the wake of the 2004 elections. The mainstream media's misguided analysis of the elections as the triumph of "traditional values" provoked the predictable range of lefty responses. Some rejected the thesis outright. Many others reaffirmed the media's conflation of Christian fundamentalism with religion by rejecting both in one fell swoop.

Sojourners editor Jim Wallis has long argued against this type of "secular fundamentalism," which cedes the terrain of religion entirely to the Republicans, leaving them free to define faith narrowly and expediently as an opposition to homosexuality and abortion.

Progressives rarely speak publicly about religion except when it's a "problem"—as in areas such as school prayer, abortion, and contraception. The academics, writers, and organizational leaders who represent our positions in the media are usually well-educated white folks who tend to be uncomfortable—and often unfamiliar—with religion. Their response to Christian fundamentalism is to oppose all faith-based politics per se. The message: any discussion of religion in the political arena is illegitimate.

The kind of knee-jerk thinking that equates faith with delusion was evident in reactions to a *New York Times* article on the role of faith in the Bush administration titled "Without a Doubt." When an aide was quoted as telling the writer, Ron Suskind, that Suskind belonged to the "reality-based community," many progressive readers were only too eager to believe that the Bush administration's deep denial of its problems was a natural corollary of the president's religious beliefs. No one, including Suskind, bothered to clarify the fact that many people in faith-based communities have little or no problem facing reality.

Contrary to popular wisdom among lefty intellectual circles, many people of faith derive their belief in social justice and equality from their religious tradition and not in opposition to it. Take, for example, the passionate and engaged discussion on NBC's *Meet the Press*, where Jim Wallis and Al Sharpton took on both Jerry Falwell and the Southern Baptist Convention's Richard Land over the definition of Christian values. By the end of the program, Wallis and Sharpton had made powerful religious arguments for public welfare, for a woman's right to choose, and for the antiwar movement. They were far more effective in undermining the Christian conservative positions on these issues than, say, the president of NOW.

This antireligious position is at odds with not just Bible Belt Americans but also vast numbers of Democrats—especially of color—who are devout believers. Writing for *Salon*, Z. Z. Packer describes the arrogant indifference of party and movement elites toward the religious Democrats such as her black evangelical mother because of her views on abortion and gay marriage. Packer's mother was "frustrated at every turn by the lack of support and infrastructure for religious lefties to engage in community outreach," Packer wrote. "What we Democrats need is our own political brand of evangelism. The conservatives have a well-wrought message, but no works. We have the substantive works, but no message, and certainly no overarching vision."

Progressives will never be able to counter Christian fundamentalism with antireligious secularism, more so because it violates our own values of tolerance and respect. Faith is an important force in the lives of most human beings, including Americans. When we treat the Church—the temple, the synagogue, or the mosque—with disdain or indifference, we do the same to its parishioners. Over the next four years, the progressive movement will face the daunting challenge of opposing both the excesses of the power-drunk Christian right and the religious opportunism of the Democratic leadership. To win, we'll need faith on our side.

Speaking Values

The truth is that there is no red state or blue state. The fiercely divisive and partisan politics of our time has served to obscure the fundamental consensus over basic values that have shaped this country. The greatest successes of the left—from the New Deal to the civil rights movement—appealed to American values of equality, justice, and compassion. The political failures of the progressive movement are not the result of a lack of moral values, as the Republicans are so fond of claiming. They reflect instead the gap between our values and the way we speak about them.

Progressives have ceded three of the most powerful words in the American vocabulary to the right: *God, family,* and *country.* The Republicans were free to use the word *patriotism* to their advantage after 9/11 because there was no competing definition of the word in people's minds. In shunning its use, we had affirmed the definition of *patriotism* as flag-waving jingoism—a mistake that we would later begin to address in our protests against the Patriot Act with banners that read "Dissent Is Patriotic."

Over and again, we have paid a heavy political price for simply ignoring or rejecting key cultural concepts rather than redefining their meaning to reflect our values. Take marriage, for example. Progressives had little to say about marriage—except for some feminist writing rejecting its value as a patriarchal institution— until gay rights groups rallied for the right to marry. Our credibility on gay marriage was undermined by our unwillingness to consistently defend the institution as valuable and meaningful for all people, gay or straight.

Progressives also need to pay greater attention to the language we use to express our values. Republican phrases, such as *special treatment* to knock affirmative action, are effective because they speak to the shared ideas of fairness and equal opportunity. Progressives instead tend to fall back on the language of rights—right to choose, right to economic security, right to clean air—which merely adds to popular misconceptions of liberal self-entitlement. While rights are important, so are the other words in the American vocabulary: *opportunity, work, freedom, equality, justice,* and *personal responsibility.*

As we work to build a new movement for change, let's remind ourselves anew that our values are American values. Let's remind ourselves that just as there are all kinds of Americans, there are all kinds of progressives.

Overcoming Liberal Contempt for the American Electorate

MICHAEL LERNER

Rabbi Michael Lerner is the editor of *Tikkun* magazine, author of several books including *Spirit Matters* and *Healing Israel/Palestine*, and co-chair of the Tikkun Community, a national interfaith peace and social justice organization (www.tikkun.org). The following is an excerpt from an e-mail he sent out after the 2004 elections.

The vast majority of liberals and progressives had the choice of who to select to run for [p]resident. They could have selected . . . Kucinich or Dean, or they could have found and drafted another candidate. They could have selected a candidate who actually reflected their own worldview. But instead they didn't—they selected someone who had voted for the war and still maintained that the war was the right thing to do, only that Bush had not run it correctly.

Polls indicated that over 68 percent of Democrats thought the war was fundamentally wrong.

Yet they selected a candidate who didn't hold that position. Why? The reason they selected Kerry, they quite openly proclaimed, is that they imagined that "the other," those Americans who were not smart enough or good enough to share our moral opposition to the war in Iraq, would vote for Kerry because he could be presented as a tough military man with a strong background in fighting the war in Vietnam. . . .

Privately, they told themselves and each other the following: Kerry is really not for this war. Once he is elected he will, we hope, feel less pressure to be opportunistic, and then the real John Kerry, the one who testified against the war in Vietnam once he came home from that war, will re-emerge and save us from this war.

In short, what liberals were saying was: This guy is an opportunist, and that's why we are for him. . . . He's just saying all this stuff to fool the American majority, but once in office, he'll (we pray and fervently hope) flip-flop and do the opposite of what he is saying now, because if he really would stick with what he is saying it would be terrible.

Please understand the contempt for the American public conveyed in this. Liberals were saying: We can trick these others into voting for someone who we ourselves don't believe stands for what he says he stands for.

And the response of the Republicans was very effective: This guy is a flip-flopper and you don't ever know where he really stands, and our proof is that his own supporters actually think there is a good chance he will flip-flop once in office. Our side has the integrity of really meaning what it is saying, but the liberals don't have that integrity.

So why did liberals follow this path? Because they deeply, deeply, deeply believe that if they were to ever present their own highest vision of a good world and a good society, the American public would reject it and then they'd be out of power. So they have to lie to the American public, based on the assumption that they are too stupid or too evil (racist, sexist, homophobic, militarist, or authoritarian) to ever respond to a really visionary progressive perspective.

And in the short run, they might be right that they wouldn't win with a more visionary perspective, because for so long the American public has heard only mush from them that it will take some time to convince them of a different vision. The right was in this situation in the 1960s, and yet it chose a different path. Instead of having a group like the Democratic Leadership Council to pull their party further and further to the center, the right said: We will stick with our ideological position, make it clearer and more easy to understand, but in some ways make it more intellectually coherent and more clearly based on some key principles, and we will be prepared to lose elections but will use those to educate the public to our perspective. And within 16 years it worked. But the liberals have never had the backbone to do that, to articulate and stick with their own most visionary perspective—and that lack of backbone is precisely why so many Americans don't respect liberals.

The Faith Factor

Barbara Ehrenreich is a social critic and essayist who writes regularly for *The Nation*, *The Progressive*, and the *New York Times*. Her most recent book, *Nickel and Dimed: On (Not) Getting By in America*, was a national best-seller. The following is an excerpt from her column published in *The Nation* in November 2004.

BARBARA EHRENREICH

Of all the loathsome spectacles we've endured since November 2, none are more repulsive than that of Democrats conceding the "moral values" edge to the party that brought us Abu Ghraib.

With their craven, breast-beating response to Bush's electoral triumph, leading Democrats only demonstrate how out of touch they really are with the religious transformation of America. Where secular-type liberals and centrists go wrong is in categorizing religion as a form of "irrationality," akin to spirituality, sports mania and emotion generally. They fail to see that the current "Christianization" of red-state America bears no resemblance to the Great Revival of the early 19th century, an ecstatic movement that filled the fields of Virginia with the rolling, shrieking and jerking bodies of the revived.

In contrast, today's right-leaning Christian churches represent a coldly Calvinist tradition in which even speaking in tongues, if it occurs at all, has been increasingly restricted to the pastor. What these churches have to offer, in addition to intangibles like eternal salvation, is concrete, material assistance. They have become an alternative welfare state, whose support rests not only on "faith" but also on the loyalty of the grateful recipients.

Drive out from Washington to the Virginia suburbs, for example, and you'll find the McLean Bible Church, spiritual home of Senator James Inhofe and other prominent right-wingers, still hopping on a weekday night. Dozens of families and teenagers enjoy a low-priced dinner in the cafeteria; a hundred unemployed people meet for prayer and job tips at the "Career Ministry"; divorced and abused women gather in support groups. Among its many services, MBC distributes free clothing to 10,000 poor people a year, helped start an inner-city ministry for at-risk youth in DC and operates a "special needs" ministry for disabled children.

MBC is a mega-church with a parking garage that could serve a medium-sized airport, but many smaller evangelical churches offer a similar array of services—childcare, after-school programs, ESL lessons, help in finding a job, not to mention the occasional cash handout. A woman I met in Minneapolis gave me her strategy for surviving bouts of destitution: "First, you find a church." A trailer-park dweller in Grand Rapids told me that he often turned to his church for help with the rent. Got a drinking problem, a vicious spouse, a wayward child, a bill due? Find a church. The closest analogy to America's bureaucratized evangelical movement is Hamas, which draws in poverty-stricken Palestinians through its own miniature welfare state.

Mainstream, even liberal, churches also provide a range of services, from soup kitchens to support groups. What makes the typical evangelicals' social welfare efforts sinister is their implicit—and sometimes not so implicit—linkage to a program for the destruction of public and secular services.

This year the connecting code words were "abortion" and "gay marriage": To vote for the candidate who opposed these supposed moral atrocities, as the Christian Coalition and so many churches strongly advised, was to vote against public housing subsidies, childcare and expanded public forms of health insurance. While Hamas operates in a nonexistent welfare state, the Christian right advances by attacking the existing one.

Of course, Bush's faith-based social welfare strategy only accelerates the downward spiral toward theocracy. Not only do the right-leaning evangelical churches offer their own, shamelessly proselytizing social services; not only do they attack candidates who favor expanded public services—but they stand to gain public money by doing so. It is this dangerous positive feedback loop, and not any new spiritual or moral dimension of American life, that the Democrats have failed to comprehend. The evangelical church-based welfare system is being fed by the deliberate destruction of the secular welfare state.

In the aftermath of election '04, centrist Democrats should not be flirting with faith but re-examining their affinity for candidates too mumble-mouthed and compromised to articulate poverty and war as the urgent moral issues they are. Jesus is on our side here, and secular liberals should not be afraid to invoke him. Policies of pre-emptive war and the upward redistribution of wealth are inversions of the Judeo-Christian ethic, which is for the most part silent, or mysteriously cryptic, on gays and abortion. At the very least, we need a firm commitment to public forms of childcare, healthcare, housing and education—for people of all faiths and no faith at all. Secondly, progressives should perhaps rethink their own disdain for service-based outreach programs. Once it was the left that provided "alternative services" in the form of free clinics, women's health centers, food co-ops and inner-city multi-service storefronts. Enterprises like these are not substitutes for an adequate public welfare state, but they can become the springboards from which to demand one.

One last lesson from the Christians—the ancient, original ones, that is. Theirs is the story of how a steadfast and heroic moral minority undermined the world's greatest empire and eventually came to power. Faced with relentless and spectacular forms of repression, they kept on meeting over their potluck dinners (the origins of later communion rituals), proselytizing and bearing witness wherever they could. For the next four years and well beyond, liberals and progressives will need to emulate these original Christians, who stood against imperial Rome with their bodies, their hearts and their souls.

The Democrats' Religion Problem

Reverend Jim Wallis is the founder of the progressive Christian magazine *Sojourners*. The following is an excerpt from an article in the magazine.

JIM WALLIS

Conventional wisdom holds that the Republicans do get "moral values" and the Democrats don't. One major reason is that Republicans are much more comfortable talking about religious values and issues and promising that their faith will impact their policies.

The Democrats, on the other hand, seem visibly uncomfortable with the subject of religion, preferring the vague language of "values"—and even then are hard-pressed to say what their values actually mean. The Democratic candidates shy away from the topic of religion and promise, as John Kerry, Howard Dean, and John Edwards have put it, that while they might have faith, it won't affect their public policies. What? It seems the Democrats are offering a totally private faith with no implications for political life. But what kind of faith is that? Where would we be if Rev. Martin Luther King Jr. had kept his faith to himself? . . .

With Democrats sitting on the religious sidelines and failing to comprehend the questions of faith, Republicans are allowed to define the "religious issues" in narrow ways that . . . benefit [primarily] them. It means the "religious issues" in this election were reduced to the Ten Commandments in public courthouses, marriage amendments, prayer in schools, and, of course, abortion. What happened to the biblical imperatives for social justice, the God who lifts up the poor, and the Jesus who says he will judge us, and the nations, by how we care for "the least of these"? How a candidate deals with poverty is a religious issue, and the Bush administration's failure to support poor working families should be named as a religious failure. Fighting pre-emptive and unilateral wars based on false claims is also a religious issue—Iraq was not a "just war" in theological terms. Neglect of the environment is another serious religious issue. . . .

Rather than suggesting we stay away from issues like "God," the Democrats should be arguing for economic security, quality health care, educational opportunity, and a just foreign and military policy on moral and religious grounds—that true faith means a compassionate concern for those left behind.

But the Democratic candidates seem to want to convince us they are entirely "secular" and speak only of the separation of church and state when the issue of religion comes up. Most Americans support that, but the separation of church and state does not require banishing moral and religious values from the public square. On the contrary, the social fabric depends on such values and vision to impact our politics. It is indeed possible (and necessary) to express one's faith in ways that are inclusive and not exclusive, that shape one's convictions about public policy while respecting the pluralism of American democracy.

There is a long history of religious faith under-girding progressive causes and movements in American history. From the abolition of slavery, women's suffrage, and civil and human rights to peace and the environment, prophetic religion has led the way to social change. But the current crop of Democrats don't seem to know that history. They had better learn it fast.

Reprinted with permission from *Sojourners*. 1-800-714-7474. www.sojo.net. *Sojourners* retains rights to the above material.

ECONOMIC POPULISM

3 ———————————————

The New Economic Populism
LAKSHMI CHAUDHRY

I t really is Michael Moore versus Mel Gibson," said former House Speaker Newt Gingrich, summing up the Republican Party's analysis of the 2004 elections. In the days after the election, Republicans were unanimous in declaring George Bush's success at the voting booth a triumph for cultural conservatism. Progressives, however, were less convinced.

Did progressives lose because we foolishly assumed people would vote their economic interests rather than their values? The answer is a resounding yes from the likes of Adam Werbach and Jim Wallis. But many others see the values card as an effective ploy that worked precisely because the Democrats failed to appeal to the "real" interests of working-class Americans. According to this line of reasoning, the GOP's success in creating cultural wedge issues is a corollary of the Democratic Party's failure to address ordinary people's economic problems—low wages, lost jobs, and lack of health care. "I disagree totally that people will deliberately vote against their economic interests when they have a lever to pull in favor of their economic interests," says Jim Hightower. "Those people did not have their economic self-interests appealed to in this campaign."

Even Thomas Frank, who takes the Democratic Party to task for ignoring the culture wars, sees the Republican version of social populism—which pits "authentic" blue-collar Americans against uppity, elitist liberals—as a covert and self-serving guise for the rhetoric of class warfare. The most persuasive answer to backlash politics, he says, is not just talking morals but offering Americans the "real deal": economic populism. In its scramble to reach out to supposed moderates, the Democratic Party, he says, has abandoned the most potent narrative—*the people versus the powerful*—in its arsenal.

Over the past three decades, the party has indeed responded to the Republican challenge by moving rightward on economic issues. The strategy is a consequence of a number of factors. One, in its race to keep up with the Republican Party in campaign fundraising, the party has grown just as addicted to large corporate donors, who are unlikely to endorse any brand of class rhetoric. Two, support for the Democratic Party continues to grow among urban, well-educated professionals, whose motivating issues tend to be social—for example, abortion rights—rather than economic. Finally, the same class of professionals today also dominates the party leadership. If you want to know why the stereotype of the latte-sipping liberal is so hard to shake, just take a look at DNC operatives on TV. It's no wonder that for the past two presidential elections, the party has selected two blue-blooded candidates with little or no ability to communicate with the average working stiff. Progressives are quick to decry the faux populism of George Bush, but in recent years the Democrats have not cared enough about ordinary Americans to even fake it.

Status Quo Liberalism

The long-term effects of the Democratic Party's economic right turn are now apparent in voting patterns among working-class Americans, especially in the so-called red states. The Democratic Achilles' heel first became apparent when blue-collar workers switched party allegiances for the first time in generations to vote Ronald Reagan into the White House. By the 1980s, Republicans had put in place a self-reinforcing feedback loop that ensured their hold over vast swathes of Middle America. The worse things got in Peoria, the more they blamed the elitist liberals in New York and San Francisco.

This feedback loop, however, required more than residual anger at the '60s counterculture to gain its strength. Americans first had to lose faith in the two pillars of the liberal economic philosophy: labor unions and government. The Reagan administration marked the beginning of a series of antilabor legislation aimed at destroying a union's right to negotiate, collect dues, or even exist. Without labor unions to remind them of the benefits of voting for Democrats—benefits that became increasingly difficult to perceive as the party embraced free-trade treaties such as NAFTA—blue-collar workers were left open to appeals that tapped into their anger at social elites.

During the same period, the conservative movement launched a multipronged campaign to persuade Americans to see government as an unnecessary burden, and the New Deal and Great Society programs as wasteful tax-and-spend liberalism.

The response of the Democratic Party to this all-out assault on its core values can be summed up in one word: appeasement. As conservatives pushed the national debate rightward on issues such as welfare, free trade, and deregulation, the Democratic presidential candidates were only too happy to adopt GOP rhetoric for electoral gain. When Bill Clinton declared in 1992, "The age of big government is over," he put the seal on the right's ideological triumph.

The more egregious failure of the Democratic Party—and of the progressive movement—has been its unwillingness to embrace change. Much has changed since Lyndon Johnson first introduced the Great Society programs. Old-fashioned U.S. multinationals that brought their profits back home have been replaced by truly global entities able to move operations and investments at will. Wall Street is now driven by forces that are beyond any one nation's control. The same Americans who once raged against Japanese cars in the '80s don't give a second thought to the "Made in China" labels on the items in their shopping bags.

Yet in all this time the Democratic Party's platform has been pretty much the same: defend the status quo against the GOP. In an online interview published on the blog MyDD (www.mydd.com), former senator Gary Hart summed up the Democratic strategy:

What happened after the '60s and into the '70s was that Democrats fell into a more or less reactionary position of trying to protect the programs that had been achieved in the period between the New Deal and the Great Society: social progressive legislation in job creation, protection of the rights of workers, urban redevelopment and so forth. When the country began to move rightward in the '70s in the pre-Reagan age, the Democrats increasingly found themselves in a position of fighting against change to protect the programs they had achieved in that 30–35 year period in the middle of the century.

Meanwhile, the Republicans had plenty of room to present themselves as the party of change. Conservatives are now free to sell their pro-corporate agenda as "reform," while progressives ironically speak of "conserving" existing programs. In 2004, the Democratic Party did not offer voters a bold new perspective on the problems of the twenty-first century, from retirement security to the Wal-Martization of America to outsourcing. John Kerry instead ran as the anti-Bush, hoping that a scathing critique of the Republican agenda accompanied by a string of damning statistics would serve as a substitute for vision.

Sympathetic critics of the progressive movement, such as Adrian Wooldridge, coauthor of *The Right Nation*, argue that the Democratic Party must do the hard work of crafting a new economic philosophy based on its core values rather than its electoral calculations. "One of the things that's gone wrong with liberalism is that instead of being very clear about what your ideals are and working from your ideals to a set of policies, you start off with a sense of what the interest groups are in your party and then tailor your policies to fit those interest groups," says Wooldridge. The result is piecemeal policymaking but no overarching vision to address the economic realities of our time.

Toward a New

The debate of values versus economic interests is a **Populism** disagreement over emphasis rather than substance. Clearly, the Republican economic agenda is not just unsustainable but also immoral. And a moral progressive vision must recognize that bread-and-butter issues are intimately connected to matters of the soul. Economic populism is based on the moral values of fairness and equal opportunity, while poverty, as progressive churches argue, ought to be an important issue for all Christians. So the challenge of crafting a new economic vision that reflects our values is just as much a moral task as it is a political necessity.

While the basic frame of economic populism—*the people versus the powerful*—holds more true than ever, the policies of a new Democratic/progressive platform must offer bold, new thinking in three core areas: the global economy, education, and the role of government.

Let's take the global economy first. All the Seattles in the world cannot put the globalization genie back in the bottle. We instead need to figure out how to make the current economic system work for ordinary working folks in the United States and around the world. This requires new thinking, especially on the domestic front. The traditional version of economic populism was influenced by blue-collar America's long-standing opposition to immigration and outsourcing, i.e., the mobility of both capital and labor.

John Kerry's position on outsourcing—he used the word repeatedly even when speaking of Iraq—tried to capitalize on popular anger at job losses, but without offering a real solution. While his proposal to end tax incentives to corporations that move jobs out of the country was morally on target, no one believed it would reverse the trend. The benefits of shipping jobs to China or India are simply too great to be offset by any carrot or stick in the federal government's arsenal. It is no different with immigration, whether we're talking about H-1B workers or illegal farm workers.

Even union leaders can read the writing on the wall. The Service Employees International Union president Andy Stern didn't pull any punches at the union's convention in 2004: "Our employers have changed, our industries have changed, and the world has certainly changed, but the labor movement's structure and culture have sadly stayed the same." While unions have already moved to embrace immigrant workers as a potential new source of membership, the task of building a global labor movement that can match the power and resources of multinational megacorporations still lies ahead.

The current form of globalization allows corporations to put profits ahead of people, both here and abroad. While Nike hires 12-year-olds to stitch shoes in Pakistan, companies in the United States are rapidly moving toward Wal-Mart's low-wage, no-benefits model.

The other part of the globalization puzzle is putting together a plan that uses new technologies as a tool to create high-skill, well-paid jobs. One such proposal has been put forth by the Apollo Alliance, which envisions strategic investments in fuel-efficient technologies that not only create jobs within the United States but also reduce consumption and decrease oil imports. Such initiatives are just small pieces of a larger economic puzzle that we need to solve in order to update liberalism for the twenty-first century.

As for education, at a time when the gap between rich and poor yawns wider than ever, this single most important guarantor of upward mobility in the United States is in a state of crisis. Despite our society's obvious failings, the American Dream retained its hold on people's imagination because our education system once offered true opportunity for all that aspired to a better life. Today, our public schools are failing and our universities have become increasingly elite institutions.

The standard progressive response on education is to call for increased spending. But spending on what? Higher salaries for teachers are important in creating a top-rate pool of educators to school our kids. However, simply plowing in more money is not going to solve the problems of the public school system, which does not prepare American kids to compete in a global labor market that values high-end technical skills. In other words, a call for genuine accountability and high standards—backed by spending guarantees—must be part of any progressive plan for education reform. We need to start thinking about how education fits into the bigger picture of economic prosperity. What a child learns today determines what kind of job he or she can hope for tomorrow.

Last, regarding the role of government, ever since the Roosevelt era, liberals have turned to the government as the panacea for economic woes. Today, however, any proposal that requires government intervention faces an uphill political battle at a time when most Americans, rightly or otherwise, believe that the government can do little to improve their lives. Our standard response to this skepticism has been to simply attack it as part of a wrong-headed and self-serving ideological agenda of the right—a tactic that has met with little success.

Part of the solution may be to commit ourselves to changing this perception, but in the interim a new progressive populism will have to envision alternative means to achieve the same ends. Lobbying for more spending on welfare, for example, is just not going to work. We may instead have to consider microfinancing small businesses to create new opportunities for inner-city families. Another approach is to use progressive organizations to offer many of the direct services that are rapidly disappearing, thanks to the GOP. Barbara Ehrenreich thinks we all can take a leaf out of the Christian right's playbook: "The progressive movement in this country is not doing enough service-based organizing. . . . We need to be creating service centers and storefronts in low-income areas [and] co-ops of different kinds, from food co-ops to credit co-ops and child-care co-ops. We don't do that."

Finally, we may have to accept the reality that there are limits to what the federal government can do today. As Adam Werbach points out, "The government doesn't have the capacity to do all the things that we want it to do. The government is not a good enough monitor of markets. It enables markets, but it can't constrain them in the way that it needs to." Besides, with the nation already saddled with a rapidly ballooning deficit, more public spending is a luxury we cannot afford in the near future.

None of this means that we should stand on the sidelines for the next four years. We must be steadfast in our opposition to this administration's plans to enrich the wealthy and the powerful at the expense of millions of Americans. But being anti-Bush didn't win us the election; it's not going to win us the wars over Social Security or public education. We must put forward brand-new alternatives to the administration's agenda that can capture the imagination of all Americans—Republican or Democrat. America is on the brink of an economic crisis. Just saying no to Bush isn't going to make it go away.

Thomas Frank, an editor of *The Baffler* magazine, shook up progressives everywhere with his eye-opening book, *What's the Matter with Kansas? How Conservatives Won the Heart of America.* Returning to his home state of Kansas, Frank set out to examine how, in recent decades, a sea of change had come about among working Kansas families, and how a whole lot of leftists had come to vote against their self-interests and to identify with conservatism and the likes of Rush Limbaugh. Frank was interviewed by Lakshmi Chaudhry in November 2004.

Interview with Thomas Frank

CHAUDHRY: So why did the Democrats lose to Bush?
FRANK: In my opinion, they consistently underestimated the phenomenon I wrote about in the book, which is the culture wars.

I don't think the strategy to deal with these things is to capitulate. You have to look at what goes on in the culture wars, understand what the subtext of it is, and figure out a way of short-circuiting it. The Democrats don't even bother, they don't think about it at all, and it's constantly surprised them.

Take, for example, the Swift Boat incident—remember those guys? Totally blindsided the Democrats. Now, how is that possible? For me, it was obvious that was going to happen—not that it would happen in that exact way, but that the Republicans would try to make an issue out of the Vietnam stuff. That they would even go to extreme, outrageous lengths to do so.

The gay marriage thing totally blindsided them. The two candidates didn't even talk about it. It was a below-the-radar effort, and yet the Republicans did talk about it at their convention, behind the scenes—that they were going to win by getting out the base with culture war appeals.

The Democrats, in response, went to their usual centrist strategy: play it right down the middle, be a very safe candidate—safe for business, safe for moderates to vote for. Essentially, it was being the non-Bush candidate, not riling up the base with the old populist rhetoric.

That's why they lost. First of all, [the Democrats] did not come up with a way of beating the culture war appeal. Second of all, they didn't rally their base. They could have done both of those things with the same strategy: being more populist in the economic sense.

CHAUDHRY: Give me an example of how you would short-circuit something like that.

FRANK: What you have to understand first is what motivates the culture wars, in each of these issues and [in] the broader cultural civil war that has gone since the late '60s. At the bottom of it all is this way of thinking and talking about social class.

Instead of it being blue collar against white collar or workers against the Fortune 500, it is average Americans—or "authentic" Americans—versus an affected liberal elite. [The Republicans] use this language of class all the time, and it is there in every single one of these issues. It's just below the surface—usually not even below the surface. It's right there.

This [class issue] was not a problem for Democrats fifty years ago. Calling Democrats an elite group back then would have been laughable. The idea of liberals being elite was ridiculous because liberals were autoworkers in Detroit, sharecroppers in Alabama. And that's who they still are, to some degree. But they have to rediscover that identity.

The Democrats have to reach out to those groups again. So you deal with that kind of upside-down class vision of the culture wars . . . by confronting it with the real deal—with real economic populism.

CHAUDHRY: One of the things that struck me is that while both Kerry and Bush were from Yale, at least the Republicans made an effort to remake Bush in this fake . . .

FRANK: Oh, right! Republicans seriously have populism on the brain. They think about it all the time. Bush is a perfect bearer of this kind of fake Republican populism. With Kerry, the Democrats weren't even thinking about it.

What's funny is that you have the two candidates from close to identical social backgrounds, even members of the same secret fraternity at Yale, okay? And one of them [Bush] comes off as this man of the people. The other comes off as this distant aristocrat, with his yacht, his mansion, his heiress wife, and his affected taste. And he can speak French.

CHAUDHRY: So what do we do with the Democratic Party? Do we abandon it? Do we remake it? Do we take it over?

FRANK: We have to take it over. There's no choice because of the way the system is set up in this country. There are a few states where you could do third-party activities, like New York State, where third-party activities are very successful. But in other states, after the populist outbreak in the 1890s, they passed laws against it. It's not illegal to have a third party [in the states], but it's effectively impossible.

Now, if you can change the law—and these are state laws—third-party efforts are a very good idea. But short of that, you have to work within the Democratic Party.

CHAUDHRY: Going beyond the party, what should we be thinking about in terms of building a new progressive movement? What are the strengths we have right now, and what do we really need to rethink? What issues are key?

FRANK: The big mistake over the [p]ast twenty to thirty years has been the movement of the Democrats to the right on the economic issues. This has been very counterproductive. I'm not saying everything Clinton did was wrong or that we have to embrace some silly agenda from the 1970s. I'm not sure precisely what we have to do, but I can tell you that things like NAFTA were a terrible mistake.

So that's key: you have to be able to speak . . . as the advocate for working people. You have to be able to do it convincingly or else you won't even get to square one.

Two, you have to rebuild your grassroots movement. If you don't have a labor movement, you don't have a left, period. The Democrats have allowed the labor movement to wither. There are a lot of reforms that could have passed in the Clinton years, when they had both houses of Congress and the presidency. They had about two years like that and they did nothing.

You have to make it easy and attractive for people to join unions. It shouldn't be this exotic thing, but a part of everyday life. That totally changes things.

The Republicans understand this—that it's a war about social movements. If you read a guy like Grover Norquist, it's clear that they're going to do everything they can to beat the labor movement because, ultimately, that movement is their enemy. It's what props up the Democratic Party. They're also going to go after the various millionaires that support the Democrats.

You have to build institutions in [Washington] DC and around the country: think tanks, cultural institutions—and not highbrow stuff either. But this is the game our team has been losing for decades, and one of the reasons is because of money, obviously. The one thing the Republicans have—and always had even when they couldn't win any elections—is a lot of money. So they're able to [fund institutions] like that.

They play the game very strategically, but our team does not. But there are plenty of people with money that came to the Democrats' side this time. They have to be persuaded to subsidize these operations.

So, those are three things they need to do.

CHAUDHRY: There's been a lot of talk of how we don't know what we stand for. We have a problem articulating our values because we don't know what they are. . . .

FRANK: I think . . . everybody agrees that this is one of the Democrats' central problems. This has always struck me as very odd because I know exactly what they're about: number one, equality; number two, security. I don't mean national security but economic security: security from booms and busts, security from the business cycle, security in old age, looking out for the weak.

As for equality, if you look back to the founding of this party and Andrew Jackson, this is what it's all about: equal rights for all, special privileges for none. That is fundamentally who the Democrats are.

CHAUDHRY: How do we go about communicating our message—when we talk about equality or security—when we're talking to Middle America? We have to have a story, and we don't seem to have one.

FRANK: The Democrats used to have a very obvious story—framing reality and talking about it in a way that was very powerful. That was the worker-ist worldview, the populist worldview. Remember Gore talked about it a little in his campaign—the people versus the powerful? That is potent stuff, and it rings true for people. They know what you're talking about.

I didn't like Bill Clinton very much, but in 1992 that was the message of the campaign he ran, and it was successful. This is what made the Democrats the majority party in the first place. The problem is that the Republicans have been able to steal this.

CHAUDHRY: We also now live in the post-9/11 era, and terrorism was an important factor in the election. How has that shifted the political terrain that liberals have to contend with?

FRANK: After 9/11 happened—I didn't write about this in the book—I said to myself, this is going to be the biggest backlash issue of all time. And that's what happened. The Republicans have just fitted [the 9/11 attack] into their existing narrative.

There are right-wing books now on winning the war against terrorists and liberals—equating the two in the sense that liberals are somehow soft on terrorism. Liberals are either in some way complicit with terrorism or don't want to fight against terrorism with sufficient vigor. They just fit it into their existing way of looking at the world. The story just writes itself.

So it's not that 9/11 changed things dramatically, but that it created this extremely powerful new issue that the Republicans then could beat liberals over their heads with.

I knew the Republicans were going to capture that issue for themselves as soon as this happened. And even though there were a million reasons why we should have been able to keep that from happening, of course we didn't.

CHAUDHRY: Give me an example of how it could have gone the other way.

FRANK: National tragedies bring people together, and they give you a fertile ground for the kind of economic security message that I was referring to earlier. If you think about World War II, that is when the welfare state really started being shaped in people's minds. Roosevelt put together a board that was going to think about plans for the postwar world—not what are we going to do with Germany and Japan, but what are we going to do here at home. And they settled on—I don't have it here in front of me— the idea of a second bill of rights, an economic bill of rights.

It's not well known anymore and most of it never got passed. But the point is that this was considered a mandate of the war. We were never going to go back to the old insecure system. When people feel . . . [the] kind of solidarity that they felt after 9/11, these kinds of ideas come naturally to mind.

Well, they didn't this time [*laughs*]. Instead, it was all about privatizing Social Security. We are going exactly the opposite way. Bush is going to hand that sucker over to Wall Street.

CHAUDHRY: So what is the average progressive—an ordinary citizen— supposed to do?

FRANK: My colleagues at *The Baffler* used to have this one-word answer: organize. This is what's wrong with Democrats. We're not out there in the streets in Middle America. We're in the media; we're in academia. We have to recover our roots.

One of the things that struck me while I was writing this book was this right-wing organizer I was talking to in Wichita. He was motivated by the abortion issue and just was constantly fighting for his issue. He was telling me about all the things he's done over the years to turn that city on its head. It went from being a place where Democrats had often won to being this hardcore conservative town. And that was because of the lengths to which he and his friends went—going door to door, signing people up.

That used to be something that Democrats did, not Republicans. Republicans were the rich people—they were the ones that talked with money. The Democrats were the ones signing up voters at the factory gates. So we have to be doing the same thing.

CHAUDHRY: So what can we do in terms of the conservative backlash? We can't give in to it.

FRANK: Yes, but we also have to attack it. We have to look for where the Republican coalition is weak. The Republican Party is made up of two large groups. One is the business class—that's who the Republican Party is and has always been. On the other hand, there are the "values" voters who have been roped in in recent decades. You have to point out to these two groups where their interests conflict. You just have to keep hitting that message.

They do it to us all the time. For example, environmentalists and labor groups. Most of their interests are the same, but they're culturally very different. Environmentalists tend to be upper middle class, while labor always tends to be working class. Republicans are constantly trying to stir up battles between them, as with the spotted owl business. And it works. We have to do it right back to them.

CHAUDHRY: In terms of opportunity for that kind of strategy, is there a danger that the Bush administration will move so far to the right— thanks to the evangelicals—as to provoke a backlash of their own?

FRANK: Will they go too far and turn the public against them? Only if we are ready with a message that's ready to make that happen.

The classic narrative is that the Democrats went too far in the 1960s. I'm not willing to admit that, because obviously the

Weathermen were not the Democrats. But however you want to look at it, the Republicans were there with a message that rang true for a lot of people. And we're still living with that today—now it's really come into its own.

So of course they're overreaching. They're frightening people. And if they get their way on *Roe v. Wade*, it will make them extremely unpopular. But we have to be standing by. We have to be ready to kick their ass. And I'm ready. Hey, I'm ready to go. Wind me up and turn me loose [*laughs*]. But the Democrats have to be ready too.

Interview with Jim Hightower

Jim Hightower is a radio commentator, author, speaker, and activist. He is the author of *Let's Stop Beating Around the Bush* and the best-selling *Thieves in High Places: They've Stolen Our Country and It's Time to Take It Back*. His column can be read on AlterNet and on his own Web site (www.jimhightower.com). He was interviewed by Lakshmi Chaudhry in November 2004.

CHAUDHRY: Why do you think the Democrats lost?

HIGHTOWER: Because we had a candidate who basically refused to run as a Democrat and to run at Bush. Kerry is certainly a decent guy, a smart guy, but he couldn't connect with working people if he was giving away Budweisers and Slim Jims. And aside from his rather loose and patrician manner, he didn't campaign on the populist issues that would appeal to working folks, including a lot of those working folks who are in evangelical churches and who ended up voting for Bush.

He didn't touch, for example, the corporate scandals. We have Kenneth Lay, Dick Cheney, and Dennis Klosowski as the poster boys of corporate greed and infamy. This stuff is readily available to anybody and easily translatable into political language. He didn't campaign against NAFTA, the WTO, these elements of globaloney that are ripping through entire towns and families. He didn't take on the great class divide that affects everything from who gets to go to college to who gets to go to war. These are the kinds of things that could've rallied the majority constituency, not only . . . holding on to and exciting the 30 percent of the electorate that did vote for Kerry, but also tapping into some of those that voted for Bush and increasing turnout among the 40 percent that did not vote.

CHAUDHRY: So you disagree with the idea that people will vote their values even if it runs counter to their economic self-interests?

HIGHTOWER: Well, I think that they're talking about an election without a campaign. Those people did not have their economic self-interests appealed to in this campaign. Bush appealed to their cultural populism and their resentment of elites. Kerry did not appeal to their economic populism and resentment of the real elites, of CEOs and wealth. So that's what . . . [has] to be done. I disagree totally that people will deliberately vote against their economic interests when they have a lever to pull in favor of their economic interests.

CHAUDHRY: Are there areas where we have to rethink our assumptions?
HIGHTOWER: Well, yeah, I think we make knee-jerk assumptions about who people are—like evangelical Christians, for example. They're overwhelmingly working folks and mostly low-income working folks who agreed with us on all of the economic issues. They want strong unions, they want not a minimum wage increase but a living wage, they want NAFTA and the WTO to be knocked in the head.

CHAUDHRY: Do we have a bigger vision that the average American can identify with and work for?
HIGHTOWER: We're about fairness, justice, and opportunity—that's a huge vision. That's the vision of America. That's what the world looks to America for. It's not our money or might. It's the fact that we've been striving for 225-odd years for some level of egalitarianism. Again, we haven't gotten there, but at least we've been trying for it. And that's exactly what the Bushites are dismantling. They're destroying the framework that unites us as a people—the idea of the common good—because they don't believe in it. They believe in the survival of the fittest and everybody else be damned. And so they're out to dismantle Social Security, wage and hour laws, [and] environmental protections, all of which allow us to implement our values of fairness and justice and opportunity.

All [progressive] groups embrace these values in one form or another. So I think we're strong on values. We're weak on presenting those values.

Since 1996, Andy Stern has been president of the Service Employees
International Union (SEIU), which now
has 1.8 million members and is the
fastest-growing union in the nation. Stern has been critical
of both the labor movement and the Democratic Party and
believes new thinking is needed. He was interviewed by Lakshmi Chaudhry in December
2004.

Interview with Andy Stern

CHAUDHRY: **Do you disagree with people on the left, especially with writers like Jim Hightower [and] Thomas Frank, who say Democrats need a stronger economic populist message?**
STERN: No, I don't think you can win an election on it alone, but you could definitely lose an election, . . . [and] John Kerry [was hurt] by having a party that doesn't have clear issues it stands for. It only adds to the question, . . . who is this person? What does he or she stand for? And so, even more than the specifics, people want to see someone who has core-strong convictions, and I tell you, the Democratic economic message is not strong, is not core. It's either "Let's go back to FDR and defend values that are now almost sixty years old" or "Let's be against what the Republicans are for."

I don't think average working people look at the Democratic Party and say, "I know what they stand for, in terms of changing my everyday economic life." I can't tell you where they stand . . . in [terms of] changing the everyday economic lives of all the workers in our union. So I think it only just adds to [the question], who is this person, what does he actually believe in? People are looking for dif-ferent kinds of choices and do live in the world where they change jobs much more frequently, and they do have a health-care crisis that's raging out of control but aren't looking for a single-payer national health-care system as a solution. There's a desperate need for a clear Democratic economic message that appeals to workers, not to entrepreneurs, venture capitalists, and intellectuals.

CHAUDHRY: What is an effective union strategy given that we're living in a highly globalized economy?

STERN: First of all, we have a global economy. We're not going to stop it—it's here. It exists and it's getting bigger and stronger. The questions are: What are its rules? How is it regulated? How do workers benefit, whether they be blue or white collar? The solution is not to go back and try to say we should have closed the borders or that NAFTA was a bad idea. The question now is whether we can change NAFTA.

So you just have to suspend history as an anchor and make it more of a guidepost. You have to integrate it with what's happening in today's world. So then the question is, how do you have global unions when you have global employers? How do you have global institutions that not just protect patents of big corporations but also protect the environment and wages? So we're just not protecting property, we're protecting people.

CHAUDHRY: So what are the basic premises of a retooled strategy?

STERN: The labor movement was created appropriately [for its time]. We had local employers—whether they were in construction or hotels [or] phone companies—that then went on to be, in many cases, regional, national, and now international. Unfortunately, we have not been growing in proportion to these enterprises. So we're falling farther and farther behind because they are changing in nature, and because we represent fewer and fewer workers in the private sector. Had we done nothing differently, companies becoming global makes us—the U.S. part—the smaller part of their overall enterprise. And that in itself makes us less strong in dealing with them. So you have to start with a premise: we need global unions to deal with global employers.

CHAUDHRY: You have talked about taking on Wal-Mart. What do you have in mind?

STERN: Wal-Mart is the largest employer not only in our country but around the world. This is about what our world is going to do about the Wal-Mart business model, which is low prices on steroids.

So we want to change their business model. In order to do that we clearly need to build coalitions with workers, environmentalists, small businesses, big businesses—all people who see the Wal-Mart business model as irresponsible. At the same time, we hope that the AFL-CIO and the UFCW—the main union in the industry—will focus their energy on getting Wal-Mart workers into unions in spite of some very difficult odds posed by a very aggressive antiunion employer.

CHAUDHRY: How do we resolve the tensions within the Democratic Party between blue-collar and white-collar workers, be it over globalization or social versus economic issues?

STERN: I have a tremendous fear that we're going to have a progressive movement that's based entirely on social issues. What we need is the kind of progressive movement that judges itself at the end of the day not only on what we do for our environment, but also on what happens to people who go to work everyday. America is not just about freedom, but also about being the land of opportunity.

The Democratic Party does have core values about choice and about rights for all people. Those are good values, but you don't win elections on those values. You win elections by building a majority. The majority of people are not white-collar, intellectual people living in urban areas that make $50,000 a year. Building a majority comes from bringing in single women, folks in the working class, people with families raising kids.

What do we have that reaches out to people whose real issues in life are how to put a decent meal on the table, get health care for their family, take care of their mother, or pay for their prescriptions? Those are the issues that most Americans deal with everyday.

CHAUDHRY: Let's do a little Monday-morning quarterbacking regarding the elections. What would you have done then, given what you know now?

STERN: I'd change the primary process. I don't think the primary process is geared toward finding candidates who can win in the states that are significantly contested: Ohio, Wisconsin, Colorado, Nevada, [and] Florida. Our process is not geared appropriately toward the general election, so the candidates who can do terrific retail politics in Iowa or New Hampshire may not be the candidates who can win in a general election, because the general election isn't about retail politics. The election is much more about impressions and media, so a) I'd change the primary process, and b) I'd ensure that the work done for the 2004 election—effective voter registration drives and then talking to voters about issues—is really institutionalized. Until now, the Democratic Party has been unable to maintain an infrastructure or organization that could talk to voters regularly. We need a permanent effort, like the Republicans have, to register voters, talk to them, and get them aware of the issues. And not at the eleventh hour, not just ninety days before an election.

CHAUDHRY: So you're saying it's all about retail politics—maybe we should define retail politics first.
STERN: I think it's very important that a candidate be able to relate to individual people, but relating to people one-on-one is only one strength. Relating to people on television, during a radio interview, at a campaign event—situations where you don't get the time for people to really know you—is even more important. There's a public identity and then there's a one-on-one identity in any relationship. I would say that if John Kerry could've talked to every voter, one-on-one, he might have been as successful nationally as he was in Iowa.

The Death of
MICHAEL **Environmentalism**
SHELLENBERGER AND TED NORDHAUS

Michael Shellenberger and Ted Nordhaus rocked the environmental world when they unveiled their paper, "The Death of Environmentalism," in September 2004 at a meeting of the Environmental Grantmakers Association. The following is an excerpt from that paper, which makes the case that environmentalism is no longer capable of dealing with the world's most pressing ecological crises. The authors call for a more visionary and inspiring progressive movement to take its place. The full essay can be read at www.theBreakthrough.org.

Those of us who were children during the birth of the modern environmental movement have no idea what it feels like to really win big.

Our parents and elders experienced something during the 1960s and 1970s that today seems like a dream: the passage of a series of powerful environmental laws too numerous to list, from the Endangered Species Act to the Clean Air and Clean Water Acts to the National Environmental Policy Act. Experiencing such epic victories had a searing impact on the minds of the movement's founders. It established a way of thinking about the environment and politics that has lasted until today.

It was also then, at the height of the movement's success, that the seeds of failure were planted. The environmental community's success created a strong confidence—and in some cases bald arrogance—that the environmental protection frame was enough to succeed at a policy level. The environmental community's belief that their power derives from defining themselves as defenders of "the environment" has prevented us from winning major legislation on global warming at the national level.

We believe that the environmental movement's foundational concepts, its method for framing legislative proposals, and its very institutions are outmoded. Today environmentalism is just another special interest. Evidence for this can be found in its concepts, its proposals, and its reasoning. What stands out is how arbitrary environmental leaders are about what gets counted and what doesn't as "environmental." Most of the movement's leading thinkers, funders and advocates do not question their most basic assumptions about who we are, what we stand for, and what it is that we should be doing.

Environmentalism is today more about protecting a supposed "thing"—"the environment"—than advancing the worldview articulated by Sierra Club founder John Muir, who nearly a century ago observed, "When we try to pick out anything by itself, we find it hitched to everything else in the Universe."

Thinking of the environment as a "thing" has had enormous implications for how environmentalists conduct their politics. The three-part strategic framework for environmental policy-making hasn't changed in forty years: first, define a problem (e.g., global warming) as "environmental." Second, craft a technical remedy (e.g., cap-and-trade). Third, sell the technical proposal to legislators through a variety of tactics, such as lobbying, third-party allies, research reports, advertising, and public relations.

When environmental leaders are asked how we can accelerate our efforts against global warming, most point to this or that tactic—more analysis, more grassroots organizing, more PR.

Few things epitomize the environmental community's tactical orientation to politics more than its search for better words and imagery to "reframe" global warming. Lately the advice has included: a) don't call it "climate change" because Americans like change; b) don't call it "global warming" because the word "warming" sounds nice; c) refer to global warming as a "heat trapping blanket" so people can understand it; d) focus attention on technological solutions—like fluorescent light bulbs and hybrid cars.

Each of these recommendations has in common the assumption that a) the problem should be framed as "environmental" and b) our legislative proposals should be technical.

Even the question of alliances, which goes to the core of political strategy, is treated within environmental circles as a tactical question—an opportunity to get this or that constituency—religious leaders! business leaders! celebrities! youth! Latinos!—to take up the fight against global warming. The implication is that if only X group were to become involved in the global warming fight[,] then things would really start to happen.

The arrogance here is that environmentalists ask not what we can do for non-environmental constituencies but what non-environmental constituencies can do for environmentalists. As a result, while public support for action on global warming is wide[,] it is also frighteningly shallow.

The environmental movement's lack of curiosity about the interests of potential allies depends on it never challenging the most basic assumptions about what does and doesn't get counted as "environmental." Because we define environmental problems so narrowly, environmental leaders come up with equally narrow solutions. In the face of perhaps the greatest calamity in modern history, environmental leaders are sanguine that selling technical solutions like fluorescent light bulbs, more efficient appliances, and hybrid cars will be sufficient to muster the necessary political strength to overcome the alliance of neoconservative ideologues and industry interests in Washington, D.C.

The entire landscape in which politics plays out has changed radically in the [p]ast thirty years, yet the environmental movement acts as though proposals based on "sound science" will be sufficient to overcome ideological and industry opposition. Environmentalists are in a culture war whether we like it or not. It's a war over our core values as Americans and over our vision for the future, and it won't be won by appealing to the rational consideration of our collective self-interest.

We have become convinced that modern environmentalism must die so that something new can live. Those of us who pay so much attention to nature's cycles know better than to fear death, which is inseparable from life. In the words of the Tao Ti Ching, "If you aren't afraid of dying[,] there is nothing you can't achieve."

Global Warming

What do we worry about when we worry about global warming? Is it the refugee crisis that will be caused when Caribbean nations are flooded? If so, shouldn't our focus be on building bigger sea walls and disaster preparedness?

Is it the food shortages that will result from reduced agricultural production? If so, shouldn't our focus be on increasing food production?

Is it that the potential collapse of the Gulf Stream, which could freeze upper North America and northern Europe, could trigger, as a recent Pentagon scenario suggests, world war?

Most environmental leaders would scoff at such framings of the problem and retort, "Disaster preparedness is not an environmental problem." It is a hallmark of environmental rationality to believe that we environmentalists search for "root causes" [and] not "symptoms." What, then, is the cause of global warming?

For most within the environmental community, the answer is easy: too much carbon in the atmosphere. Framed this way, the solution is logical: we need to pass legislation that reduces carbon emissions. But what are the obstacles to removing carbon from the atmosphere?

Consider what would happen if we identified the obstacles as:

- The radical right's control of all three branches of the US government.
- Trade policies that undermine environmental protections.
- Our failure to articulate an inspiring and positive vision.
- Overpopulation.
- The influence of money in American politics.
- Our inability to craft legislative proposals that shape the debate around core American values.
- Poverty.
- Old assumptions about what the problem is and what it isn't.

The point here is not just that global warming has many causes but also that the solutions we dream up depend on how we structure the problem.

The environmental movement's failure to craft inspiring and powerful proposals to deal with global warming is directly related to the movement's reductive logic about the supposedly root causes (e.g., "too much carbon in the atmosphere") of any given environmental problem. The problem is that once you identify something as the root cause, you have little reason to look for even deeper causes or connections with other root causes.

The environmental movement's technical policy orientation has created a kind of myopia: everyone is looking for short-term policy pay-off. We could find nobody who is crafting political proposals that, through the alternative vision and values they introduce, create the context for electoral and legislative victories down the road.

Political proposals that provide a long-term punch by their very nature set up political conflicts and controversy on terms that advance the environmental movement's transformative vision and values. But many within the movement are uncomfortable thinking about their proposals in a transformative political context. When we asked Hal Harvey how he would craft his energy proposals so that the resulting political controversy would build the power of environmentalists to pass legislation, Harvey replied, "I don't know if I want a lot of controversy in these packages. I want astonishment."

The marriage between vision, values, and policy has proved elusive for environmentalists. This is a crisis because environmentalism will never be able to muster the strength it needs to deal with the global warming problem as long as it is seen as a "special interest." And it will continue to be seen as a special interest as long as it narrowly identifies the problem as "environmental" and the solutions as technical.

The Apollo Alliance

In early 2003 we joined with the Carol/Trevelyan Strategy Group, the Center on Wisconsin Strategy, the Common Assets

Defense Fund, and the Institute for America's Future to create a proposal for a "New Apollo Project" aimed at freeing the US from oil and creating millions of good new jobs over ten years. Our strategy was to create something inspiring. Something that would remind people of the American dream: that we are a can-do people capable of achieving great things when we put our minds to it.

Apollo's focus on big investments into clean energy, transportation and efficiency is part of a hopeful and patriotic story that we are all in this economy together. It allows politicians to inject big ideas into contested political spaces, define the debate, attract allies, and legislate. And it uses big solutions to frame the problem—not the other way around.

Until now the Apollo Alliance has focused on building a coalition of environmental, labor, business, and community allies who share a common vision for the future and a common set of values. The Apollo vision was endorsed by seventeen of the country's leading labor unions and environmental groups ranging from NRDC to Rainforest Action Network.

Whether or not you believe that the New Apollo Project is on the mark, it is at the very least a sincere attempt to undermine the assumptions beneath special interest environmentalism. Apollo offers a vision that can set the context for a myriad of national and local Apollo proposals, all of which will aim to treat labor unions, civil rights groups, and businesses not simply as means to an end but as true allies whose interests in economic development can be aligned with strong action on global warming.

Apollo is not the whole answer to the environmental movement's losing streak on global warming. Rather, we are arguing that all proposals aimed at dealing with global warming—Kyoto, McCain-Lieberman, carbon taxes and Apollo—must be evaluated not only for whether they will get us the environmental protections we need but also for whether they will define the debate, divide our opponents and build our political power over time.

The strength of any given political proposal turns more on its vision for the future and the values it carries within it than on its technical policy specifications. What's so powerful about Apollo is not its ten-point plan or its detailed set of policies but its inclusive and hopeful vision for America's future.

Apollo was created differently from proposals like McCain-Lieberman. We started by getting clear about our vision and values and then created a coalition of environmentalists, unions, and civil rights groups before reaching out to Reagan Democrats and other blue-collar constituents who have been financially wrecked by the [p]ast twenty years of economic and trade policies. These working families were a key part of the New Deal coalition that governed America through the middle of the [p]ast century. Though ostensibly liberal on economic issues, Reagan Democrats have become increasingly suspicious of American government and conservative on social issues, including environmentalism, due in no small part to the success of conservatives in consistently targeting this group with strategic initiatives. And yet more than 80 percent of Reagan Democrats, our polling discovered, support Apollo—higher rates even than college-educated Democrats.

Apollo will be successful if it elevates the key progressive values noted above among this critical constituency of opportunity. It should be conceived of as one among several initiatives designed to create bridge values for this constituency to move toward holding consistent and coherent views that look more and more like those of America's progressive and environmental base. Apollo stresses the need for greater public-private investments to establish American leadership in the clean energy revolution— investments like those America made in the railroads, the highways, the electronics industry and the Internet.

"The first wave of environmentalism was framed around conservation and the second around regulation," says California Apollo Project member Van Jones. "We believe the third wave will be framed around investment."

Industry and the neoconservatives make proposals using their core values as a strategy for building a political majority. Liberals, especially environmentalists, try to win on one issue at a time. We come together only around elections when our candidates run on our issue lists and technical policy solutions. The problem, of course, isn't just that environmentalism has become a special interest. The problem is that all liberal politics have become special interests.

Talking about the millions of jobs that will be created by accelerating our transition to a clean energy economy offers more than a good defense against industry attacks: it's a frame that moves the environmental movement away from apocalyptic global warming scenarios that tend to create feelings of helplessness and isolation among would-be supporters.

Once environmentalists offer a compelling vision for the future, we will be in a much better position to stop being Pollyanna about the state of [our] politics. Kevin Phillips recently argued in *Harper's Magazine* that the decline of liberalism began because "liberal intellectuals and policy makers had become too sure of themselves, so lazy and complacent that they failed to pay attention to people who didn't share their opinions."

Environmentalists find themselves in the same place today. We are so certain about what the problem is, and so committed to legislative solutions, that we behave as though all we need is to tell the literal truth in order to pass our policies. We need to tap into the creative worlds of myth-making, even religion, not to better sell narrow and technical policy proposals but rather to figure out who we are and who we need to be.

Above all else, we need to take a hard look at the institutions the movement has built over the [p]ast thirty years. Are existing environmental institutions up to the task of imagining the post–global warming world? Or do we now need a set of new institutions founded around a more expansive vision and set of values? One thing is certain: if we hope to achieve our objectives around global warming and a myriad of intimately related problems, then we need to take an urgent step backwards before we can take two steps forward.

GETTING ACTIVE

WHERE TO
START

1 ——————————————————

Taking Action
DON HAZEN

This last section is for readers who want to *do something*. It offers some very practical ideas and activities for moving forward to build a better and stronger progressive movement.

Real grassroots democracy is possible only if millions of us take responsibility for making change. It is clear that a "top down" communications model, whether it be in the Democratic Party, in media corporations, or even in big liberal nongovernmental organizations (NGOs), is more about power and control than it is about pursuing the goals of fairness and social justice.

In many ways, John Kerry did the best he could during the 2004 campaign, but one of the key reasons he lost is because he was a creature of a political system and a party that had long lost touch with real people. Neither the party nor Kerry had a clear story to tell that made sense to many Americans. Kerry was a confused Democrat because he tried to straddle too many issues and didn't communicate a clear vision.

It is time to change all that. To move forward, we must invest ourselves in electoral politics in our neighborhoods, cities, and regions. It is one thing to be sick and tired of media consultants, spinners, pollsters, polls, and corporate donors controlling our lives. It is yet another thing to be willing to jump into the fray, to take the momentum that began with the 2004 election and build on it.

A revolution did get started in 2004—but it was just the first step. Whether it was Meetups, MoveOn campaigns, blogs, voter registration, satire, or do-it-yourself local politics, many of us took our first steps, but there is far more to do ahead before we can win back power.

If we want to win our country back, we can't just be angry, or simply indulge in our contempt for all things red and conservative—we need to persuade people, not push them further away.

In this section, we'll hear from Wes Boyd, the cofounder of MoveOn, about that group's ambitious plan for the future, and from Colin Greer, who has been funding grassroots activists for more than twenty-five years. Then I'll present my twelve-step program for winning progressive politics. Before we go forward, each of us should make a personal assessment of where we are and what it is we are ready to do.

The twelve steps are followed by various insightful and practical tips, important ways to make use of independent media, and finally some of the ingredients for do-it-yourself politics. Yes, there are lots of organizations to connect with, but sometimes it is more effective to organize something new and exciting yourself.

In the end, however, it is about our values: what we care about and why we are involved in the work. Let's remember that the things we believe in—equality, fairness, justice, dignity, and ultimately kindness and love—inspired some of the significant moral and political achievements of the twentieth century: civil rights legislation, equal rights for women, the right to organize, and the minimum wage. These values make our nation strong and inspiring to the rest of the world. We must protect, nourish, and build on them in the twenty-first century as well.

GETTING ACTIVE

On January 20, 2005, Inaugural Day, MoveOn (www.moveon.org) proposed a strikingly ambitious plan: to organize "networks of neighbors and friends" in every Congressional district that would together create a "national message," and to use the networks to take back the House of Representatives in 2006. In the missive sent to its 3-million-member list, the MoveOn leaders said the plan came directly from the members in terms of their comments about MoveOn's future. For many members, this was a signal that the organization had dramatically shifted gears after the Democrats' defeat in November. For Wes Boyd, cofounder, with Joan Blades, of MoveOn, the declaration represented a transition from working in support of John Kerry's presidential bid and the Democratic Party to building a true grassroots movement. Boyd was interviewed in January 2005 by Don Hazen.

Interview with Wes Boyd

HAZEN: Does this ambitious new plan represent a big shift for MoveOn? How is the membership responding?

BOYD: The reaction has been fantastic. I think that's because this plan is a natural extension of the tremendous energy of last year, but focused on a broader goal. Millions of progressives who had never before been involved in politics got busy last year working for campaigns and getting out the vote. And they liked it. They liked meeting neighbors and talking together about the future. They liked the sense of joint mission and purpose. And they want to keep moving forward. Progressive populism is a real movement now, and MoveOn is just a small part of this wave.

As our contribution to this wave, we're working to help find good ways for individuals to act at the local level as part of something big and national. The most important part of this plan is the identification of an audacious but achievable goal: organizing to sweep away the right-wing majority in Congress in 2006. It's utterly predictable that the radical right will overreach in the coming political season. Their claims of a mandate, in the face of a deeply divided electorate, make that clear. If we're ready, we can take Americans' natural aversion to extremists and take Congress in the 2006 election on a progressive reform agenda.

HAZEN: You describe hiring organizers, building infrastructure, and recruiting grassroots leaders. Who will make it happen on the ground—can you explain how this might work?

BOYD: We're starting with the model of our Leave No Voter Behind program from last year. Tens of thousands of volunteers worked at the local level with help from hundreds of paid organizers. Most political campaigns use only paid staff, including even [for] phone banking and canvassing efforts. They don't really trust volunteers. Leave No Voter Behind was a true neighbor-to-neighbor program, and the results show how powerful volunteer-driven efforts can be. The key, though, is how to set national goals together, so that everyone's efforts add up to something bigger.

HAZEN: What does it mean to develop a national message from the ground up?

BOYD: That's probably the biggest, most exciting challenge we face. It's never really been done before, but the Internet gives us new opportunities to broadly engage in these discussions and draw in the huge talent and expertise of Americans outside of Washington DC. Right after the election, MoveOn members held 1,600 house parties across the nation to talk about next steps. That was a start. Everyone agreed on one key goal: progressives need to hone a clear agenda to counter the think-tank-developed programs of the radical right. We have to get off defense and move to offense. That will take new ideas and a common embrace of key initiatives. With some innovation, a progressive agenda with broad appeal can and will emerge.

HAZEN: Getting back to the 2004 election, what's your view with 20/20 hindsight?

BOYD: I don't blame Kerry so much but rather the Democratic Party as an institution. The message just wasn't there. You can't expect a candidate to arrive in March and create something out of whole cloth. The party currently is about fund-raising and occasionally blasting out ads. The senate and congressional campaign committees keep getting more and more narrow in their targeting—there is little work done on national message. The party has to be much more. It has to connect in a real way with rank-and-file members and be their voice.

Progressives have been on defense for so long that the building blocks aren't ready to move, the strategic initiatives aren't ready to go. Bush, who certainly isn't a great leader, can, for example, pick up a strategic effort on Social Security right after the election and it's all ready to roll . . . their infrastructure is always working and always ready to move on to the next thing without pause.

HAZEN: What about the Internet? Didn't the DNC and Kerry use it effectively?

BOYD: The Democratic Party had no idea how to use the Internet. They treated it like free money and then kept on doing all the rest of the things they normally do—working to raise money from the same big contributors. They don't understand or want to use the Internet as the two-way communication system it is.

HAZEN: MoveOn created some controversy with this statement shortly after the election: "In the last year, grassroots contributors like us gave more than $300 million to the Kerry campaign and the DNC and proved that the party doesn't need corporate cash to be competitive. Now it's our party: we bought it, we own it, and we're going to take it back." What were you saying? What did you mean?

BOYD: Well sure, it should read "We the people"—it's not meant to read "We, MoveOn." But the ability for the party to gain most of its support from small contributors is nothing less than revolutionary. The Democratic rank and file can own the party because there is a way [for them] to fund-raise and support the party. This changes everything. It especially means that Democrats can stop mumbling when they speak about important issues that involve the interests of big contributors. The Democratic Party can be the populist party not just in name and reputation but in reality.

But Internet engagement of a base of support does more than bring financial support. It gives leaders another channel for engaging with real people and to understand their issues and concerns. I'm very resistant to the role of pollsters. They act in political circles like sage interpreters, the middle men between the political elite and the people. They reinforce the notion that our political leaders are separate—they are not like normal people—and some of the political elite really do look down on Americans. Pollsters tell you what kinds of coffee elites drink—lattes—[and] how that's different from the rest of Americans who drink regular coffee. That is so superficial. And it's disempowering to leaders. You can't lead unless you believe in what you are saying. Good leaders reach out to our common humanity and our better instincts. They don't pander.

HAZEN: But MoveOn used its fair share of consultants and spent a lot of money on them.

BOYD: There is a lot to learn from good political professionals. One of our strengths is in integrating the old with the new, and you can't do that unless you learn from those who have gone before. However, I would hope that we see a new model for political consultants emerge, based on the opportunities represented by the Internet and connections to the real constituencies.

HAZEN: What about the wing of the Democratic Party that wants it to move rightward, or to the middle, as they say?

BOYD: It's silly to try to move to the center. There is no center. There is no single dimension in politics. People are far too complex to classify this way. You never will see the right move to some theoretical center, because they understand that their power stems from projecting a coherent story about the problems we face and where we need to go. They are wrong, but they're coherent. They don't mumble.

We're engaged with millions of people and we can testify: there is no gravitational pull from the masses to some center. We don't avoid moving to the center because of ideology. We simply are not hearing that from America.

This reminds me of the argument about whether we should focus on the "base" or on the "average American." This is simplistic, too. There is no average American. It's a false choice. The base is the group of people who are ready to work and support leadership. To fail to engage the base is to fail to be politically effective. The base is the key to progressives engaging America more broadly. But you have to do both.

Another silly argument is the debate [about] which is more important: message or field. If you take a business perspective, you think about the question of marketing versus sales. Are you going to chose between marketing and sales? Of course not. You need both, and both have to be strong. When you look at the Democrats, they have been relatively strong in field over time but desperately weak on message. The values are there, but they haven't been developed into a coherent story and strong initiatives. And then there is the red/blue thing, another obstacle. We need to engage all of America. That has to be a political goal, not this preoccupation with targeting.

HAZEN: There has been some confusion about how much money MoveOn raised and spent in the election cycle and what you did with it. Can you help clarify?

BOYD: Well, it happened in stages. From late 2003 into the middle of 2004 the MoveOn.org 501(c)(4) raised $5 million and ran issue advocacy efforts like our Fox campaign. Then the MoveOn.org Voter Fund raised about $20 million, half of that from big donors to match small contributions and help build the small-donor base. That was spent mostly on opposition media. The MoveOn PAC then raised $5 million for Congressional candidates, and an additional $25 million was raised for programs like Leave No Voter Behind and the swing-state ad program.

HAZEN: You have taken some heat from the blogs for MoveOn being too "top down." How do you respond?

BOYD: We have a very quick and accurate feedback mechanism with our membership. We try to model a style of leadership where deep listening and reflection of the concerns of the membership are the source of our collective power and effectiveness. We see ourselves as offering a service, not . . . telling people what to do. If people appreciate the service, we'll do well and have an impact together.

HAZEN: Beltway conservatives calling for a "new liberalism" on military steroids have recently placed MoveOn in their sights. *New Republic* editor Peter Beinart called MoveOn "soft," claiming that its efforts are doomed because it does not put "the struggle against America's new totalitarian foe at the center of its hopes for a better world." What is your response?

BOYD: The idea that we should identify an entire culture as a totalitarian movement for Democrats to oppose—I think that's wrong and I think it's dangerous. We and MoveOn are keenly aware of the need for vigilance against terrorism. We do not minimize the threats we face, nor are we hostile to U.S. power or its use to counter real dangers. Security must be a guiding principle for Democrats and all Americans. We, like most Americans, want our children safe, our homes and offices secure, and terrorism defeated.

However, one of the problems is in the dynamic of opposition and the media. It's simple—we've been in the opposition and on defense for a long time. So when the president says that the way to fight terrorism is to fight a war in Iraq, we say, "Wait a second, are you insane?" That's perceived as not caring about terrorism. We know that people here, the staff and the members, care deeply about security but are looking for leaders who are ready to address the real challenges of security in the post-9/11 world.

We believe in the wisdom of crowds, and we believe that the policy elites in Washington DC get it wrong pretty damn consistently. In the end, the future of liberalism/progressivism depends not on identifying and vilifying an enemy and manipulating the American public but on espousing a positive vision for the future around which a movement, a party, and an American consensus can be built.

Interview with Colin Greer

Colin Greer is the coauthor, with Herbert Kohl, of *A Call to Character* and is a regular contributor to *Parade* magazine. Greer is also president of the New World Foundation and is an expert on funding for progressive causes. Among other things, Greer believes all funders—institutions and individuals—must shift more of the money to the local level. Greer was interviewed by Don Hazen in December 2004.

HAZEN: As a longtime funder of grassroots organizations, what did you see as the weaknesses in the 2004 campaign?

GREER: First, there is in fact no Democratic Party on the ground in most states except during a presidential campaign. So there is little infrastructure for electoral work. In this last campaign, local Democratic officials complained that they were not included in John Kerry events. Yet people are often drawn to vote through their identification with their local representatives.

The Republicans did not make that error. They have spent thirty years building an organizational base at the local and state level, running candidates for local office in well-funded and carefully chosen elections. And they do not run away from these officials in national campaign tours.

It's worth noticing that progressive activists have been doing the same locally, but without much support from national political leaders and financiers. So to recognize that Republicans have been doing it for thirty years doesn't mean we have to wait thirty years, too; instead, it means funding what's out there, helping to sustain it, grow it, and expand it.

HAZEN: What is a smart response to that problem of lack of success at the grass roots?

GREER: There is a potential infrastructure for a Democratic Party in multi-issue, community-based organizations throughout the nation. These organizations often contract to do registration and

GOTV [get out the vote] in national elections, when they are frequently overloaded with demands. They are thoroughly underfunded during the off years, however, when they could be developing and supporting candidates for city council, sheriff, judgeships, et cetera. As a result, they are weak and unpracticed each time they enter the national electoral fray.

HAZEN: Are there examples of how it might work?

GREER: Yes. In 2004 we saw what can happen at the local level: in Montana, reservation Indians helped win back the assembly; in New Mexico, Southwest Organizing Project won precincts in the hitherto Republican heartland; New Yorkers made inroads on the Republican senate majority; and supposedly red Florida and Nevada passed initiatives increasing the minimum wage. Unfortunately, the national funding in 2004 basically ignored this local capacity, except to contract with it for the last few months. And even then, the national money mostly went to bring in outside canvassers, campaign managers, et cetera, with command for the most part in the hands of white activists. What works is local and state-level activists in organizations winning electoral and policy victories. All this is under the radar of national Democratic experts. The dominant model is wrongheaded; what works is calling out to us if we would listen.

HAZEN: What's in the way?

GREER: Well, for starters all the top national people in the 2004 Democratic campaign, with one exception [Donna Brazile], were white. Many of the national intermediaries funneling money and designing registration strategy were white, and media vendors and consultants were largely white—and urban, too. Very often, their target base comprised people of color who were often rural as well. A pretty poor match.

The leadership in the community-based organization infrastructure could make an enormous difference in this area. Unfortunately, national campaign professionals didn't see it that way, and don't now in their postmortems. We are inundated by professional political advisors convinced that elections are won and sealed through the work of think tanks, rich philanthropists, and media magnates.

Clearly, we need to be working on a number of fronts. Equally clearly, we can begin a winning exodus out of the political wilderness and sustain winning through tactical smarts. If our tactical approach embraces and strengthens young people, working people, people of color, and communities all over America, each campaign is a win, even if not an electoral victory. Our organizational capacity on the ground grows in strength, along with its ability to intersect with leadership, initiatives, and ideas at the national level.

HAZEN: Looking ahead, what tactics or innovations could help change some of these "top down" dynamics and find fertile ground locally?
GREER: Well, let's take youth, for example. In 2004, youth turnout went up some. However, college youth . . . increased its turnout substantially [only] in the targeted battleground states. Voter registration and GOTV largely ignored community colleges, where the vast majority of low-income students and students of color study. Youth in community colleges need to become the focus of organizing in sustained year-in, year-out electoral work. These youths—future paraprofessionals, technicians, and professionals, disproportionately of color—can be linked in a serious and forceful partnership with community-based organizations. They are, after all, connected to those communities, and most will make their careers in the same or similar communities.

HAZEN: What about the big picture? What elements are necessary for national success?
GREER: It's important to remember that political power is not built prior to electoral victory. It grows interwoven with it. With the electorate so evenly split in so many states, we can start with well-run elections that win local campaigns. The goal is to build state-

level power that grows into a national political force, as Newt Gingrich and the Republicans did in 1994. Nationally marketable messages work best when they connect with a loyal base and directly confront a political opposition.

For thirty years, Republicans alchemized defeat into a tonic for robust, rugged, intense, and impassioned opposition politics. Democrats swallowed a wimpish, wonkish toxin that has sent them sprawling each time the lights go down on a presidential sweepstakes. We need national and local leaders to embrace a consciously oppositional identity, generating campaigns and messages that convey a sense of forceful commitment to the people whose interests they aim to represent.

Twelve-Step Program for Progressive Victories DON HAZEN

1. Take Responsibility

We must admit that we have not done the necessary work to exercise political power. Whether it is because of privilege, single-issue focus, or simply the time and effort required for success, we have not done enough. We must own the fact the conservatives have wanted to win more. If we want to end the right-wing hegemony on the federal level and in many states, we must look into the mirror and understand that it is we who must change our behaviors first. All other steps follow this basic acknowledgment.

2. Understand Our Strengths

On a personal level, make a self-assessment: What do you do well? What is your best contribution? We need a list of talents and styles and levels of engagement in research, networking, event organizing, talking about the issues, design, Web work, basic administrative support, and so on.

On a national level, a new electoral movement emerged in 2004, showing great promise; many engaged in elections for the first time. There is a powerful progressive tradition from which to draw. Recognizing our assets, we can move forward with all our strength.

3. Recognize Our Weaknesses

Progressives often repeat the same strategies and behaviors no matter how often they fail. We think the facts are going to win arguments and elections. We intellectualize our positions. We can be shrill and find it difficult to compromise. We

often do not provide a clear vision for the future. We're better on
the attack than when offering positive alternatives. It is time to
stop and rethink many of our attitudes and strategies. In the big
picture, by most measures—media, grassroots infrastructure, think
tanks—progressives are far behind the right wing.

4. Accept What We Are Powerless to Change

For instance, ever since 9/11, a lot of Americans are
susceptible to a politician playing to their fears, and there is not a
lot we can do about that. Another reality we must accept is that
many conservative fundamentalists will never agree with our
values and our goals. Yet there is no doubt that a majority of
Americans will be on our side if we clearly articulate our moral
vision.

5. Know What We Believe In

The basic progressive vision is one of community,
where people care about each other and not just themselves and
act responsibly. George Lakoff argues that core progressive values
are family values and include protection, fulfillment in life, fairness, freedom, opportunity, prosperity, service, and cooperation.
His ten-word progressive mantra is "Stronger America, broad prosperity, better future, effective government, mutual responsibility."
This formulation may not be yours, but it is a good starting point.
How would you articulate your vision and values?

6. Communicate a Positive Vision

It follows that if we know our values, we must put
forth a positive message, a set of energizing ideas that will help us
prepare and mobilize for the future. Attacking the opponents' message often reinforces it. For example, when we use the conservatives' language of "Social Security reform" or "tax relief," even
when criticizing it, we are reiterating its message. We need to communicate *our* message.

7. Know Where We Are Going

It is crucial to know what our goals are—both short term and long term. And it is important to think strategically. Is the target a local political issue, finding new candidates to run for office, building local progressive networks, winning Congress? Be clear about what your goal is and the steps necessary to reach it. Reading, being informed, and signing e-mail petitions, while good, are just not enough.

8. Reach Out to Others

Many of us have a pretty narrow political comfort zone. Talking to others who may not agree with us about specific political issues is hard. We can't win without changing minds and mobilizing the disinterested. Obviously some people can't be reached. But when you meet people unlike you, look for the common ground.

9. Be Realistic

There are no magic bullets that will create social change or win elections. Those who think that framing a more positive message is the entire answer are mistaken. There are many ingredients necessary for political success, including a positive vision, powerful ideas, effective communications, sufficient resources, committed activists, and an effective grassroots infrastructure.

10. Deal with Fear

Fear is the subtext of American politics, as was evident in 2004. Fearful people tend to vote conservative, and many Americans will be fearful of change. Progressives need to develop their positions on terrorism and to be comfortable and confident when talking about issues that frighten Americans.

11. Embrace Diversity

Like fairness and protecting our families, diversity is a fundamental progressive value and is essential to winning elections. African-Americans are the most reliable progressive voters, followed by Latinos and single women, and yet virtually all Kerry campaign officials were East Coast and white and mostly all were male, and they had a very hard time relating to working families.

12. Make a Commitment

Here is where the rubber meets the road. Get specific. How much time are you willing to commit? Can you give one hour a week? Three? More? Are you willing to allocate a certain amount of additional money each month to bring about change? How will you know whether you are using your time and energy effectively? If you truly want to push the conservatives out of power, you must do more . . . now.

ACTION REFORM

2

Kumbaya Time Again: Organizing for Success

DAN CAROL

Dan Carol is founder of Carol/Trevelyan Strategy Group. He writes regularly for his blog, Kumbaya, Dammit (www.kumbayadammit.com).

Most of us have been on an emotional roller coaster since the election, riding from rage to sadness to resigned and then back to rage again. But now things seem to be settling down—and it's time to get down to business. There are some very specific things we ought to be doing, like making electoral politics a regular, year-round activity. And clearly the time to act is now. Here is a new round of organizing principles and to-do's for the next months and onward:

GET UP . . . AND GET YOUR WAR ON. Enough moaning. This is a long struggle, and admit it, we're Americans who want instant gratification, even in our politics. This was not a 1984 or 1964 landslide. We put 56 million votes on the board and 252 electoral votes. Change takes time. Think Nelson Mandela.

STOP THE HAND-WRINGING ABOUT THE DNC, THE DLC, ET AL. The old era of political party identification is giving way to a disaggregated thunderdome of cause-based politics, distributed democracy, MoveOn, house parties, and do-it-yourself politics. Peer-to-peer politics—in churches, workplaces, schools, music clubs—is replacing the party as the place where new stuff happens. Are you ready to help build a new network for change, rather than pick fights over who runs a political party with a declining brand?

SENATORIAL SPINE: EMERGENCY INFUSION REQUIRED. Please get in the faces of our forty-four Democratic senators, from the Mary Landrieus to the Ron Wydens, and give them love, encouragement, and the gumption to stand tall against the coming Bush juggernaut. Urge them to read Thomas Frank's book *What's the Matter With Kansas?* and ask them to think hard about where "moderating" Democratic principles has gotten us. Now is not the time to lie down on economic populism.

IT'S NOT EITHER/OR; WE HAVE TO DO BOTH . . . ACTUALLY, ALL OF THE ABOVE. Yes, we need a better message. And better mechanics. We need to win over our base voters as well as those "persuadables." We need to "go big" on our thematics, yet microtarget our audiences. Every campaign struggles over these either/or choices, when the right answer is usually doing the best of both! On mechanics, we have the technology, training, and talent to effectively manage high-tech and high-touch grassroots politics. That means the third "M"—money—needs to be there.

MONEY, MONEY, MONEY. So what's with all these rich dudes who are helping the Democrats? Hats off to George Soros for jump-starting civil society here in America again. (More hats off, of course, to Howard Dean's campaign for showing the way on online fundraising.) But while it's nice that there are progressive sugar daddies and mommies, the key here is building a sustainable revenue stream for our politics through small-donor networks and a membership-based, business model (wow, it almost sounds like a new union).

MEET THE FERTILIZER FUND. How do we steer in the next ten years? Well, we have some real capacity in single-issue, cause-based groups.

Let's make sure that we nurture and network them and create new links among them. Before we create another new group or launch another new ad campaign, let's leave behind a little money to seed success for the long haul. Rich dudes, big groups, our friends in Silicon Valley and at the new Democracy Alliance—everyone— should give, at a bare minimum, 10 percent of their new money raised to organizations that provide needed infrastructure.

We know what we need (list matching, voter files, election protection) and what works (living wage, boots on the ground, a growing farm team of state and local candidates through great groups like Progressive Majority and Wellstone Action). Also needed: a new collective of smart state directors to run states, their way.

STATES: DEVOLUTION IS OUR FRIEND. Until the rules change in the electoral college, ya gotta win states to win the presidency. We will win elections when and where we can create effective state electoral networks that bring progressives and Democrats to the polls. The issue might be health care or education, or it might be some other local concern driven by a national player like SEIU, People for the American Way, the PIRGs, Sierra Club, you name it. The organizing center of that network might be the state Democratic Party, a new group like the Working Families Party in New York, or a homegrown organizing effort like the Oregon Bus Project (www.busproject.org).

In short, devolution is our friend. Because while we can't win diddly in Washington DC right now, we win all the time out in the states on issues like living wage (hello, Florida and Nevada). So let's leave behind an elite fighting force for existing federal regulations in DC and gather our strength in the hills.

WE'RE ALL GETTING ALONG, RIGHT? We do need some cultural change among our top leaders to help open new doors and share our strategic thinking more widely. So take a deep breath if this collaborative-kumbaya stuff gives you shortness of breath. If you can't work with someone, don't. But do find a way to share what you are doing, because transparency is a form of collaboration. Transparency, for progressives, is progress.

The good news is that a new generation of leaders is emerging—folks like Cecile Richards of America Votes, Mark Ritchie of National Voice, and Amy Chapman of Grassroots Democrats. Rob Stein, of the famed PowerPoint about the conservatives' media message machine matrix, is also an important new leader.

SHOW TRIALS FOR SHRUM & CO.? Of course we've spent too much in the past twenty years on Democratic TV spots while underfunding infrastructure. But let's save the show trials for the creeps who okayed the torture sessions at Abu Ghraib. The accountability I most want in politics applies to our candidates. But we can't expect party loyalty without something to discipline candidates who sell us out on key Medicare votes. At a minimum, candidates who take money from progressive PACs should sign a pledge to certain core progressive values.

MESSAGE 101: HOPE BEATS FEAR. First of all, forget the "values" debate—that's their frame, their Luntzian head game. All that Election 2004 proved is the old adage "You can't fight something with nothing." We can't beat a fear-based, Republican message with silence. The Kerry campaign failed to articulate a hopeful, national call to action in the post-9/11 era and instead offered vague "plans" under the theme of "not Bush." This is not a moral crisis for the Democrats—it's just a weak message. While we're on the values topic, I have kids, as do millions of other parent-voters, and we all wish American culture would slow down just a tad. There are plenty of ways to talk about these issues effectively: go ask Obama.

THE PERFECT MESSAGE. Guess what? There isn't one. We have lots of inspiring core beliefs to share, from faith and tolerance in our hearts to dignified retirement and childhood at home to girls' education and citizen diplomacy abroad. Whatever we call the New

American Dream, we just need to speak from the gut and articulate hope—and echo it all via the new, collaborative platform for media, entertainment, and activism now taking shape. We also need to microtarget, organize, and motivate different audiences, in different places, at different paces. This iterative approach can work, especially if we mimic the right on one score: patience. The top conservatives didn't look for one single slogan to win power in an instant or an election cycle; they crafted solid messages, organizing and executing over many years. Let's copy that.

Election Reform

Chellie Pingree is the president and CEO of Common Cause. Prior to that, she spent eight years in the Maine legislature.

CHELLIE PINGREE

By the morning of November 3, 2004, Americans knew the winner of the presidential election. But quickly knowing who won and having an election without ensuing litigation only papers over the major problems that remain with our system of voting.

Voting Problems

This much is clear: Voting in 2004 was more problematic than in 2000. Thousands of people waited in lines as long as eight hours to cast a ballot. Many thousands more were turned away at the polls due to registration issues, and still thousands more who requested absentee ballots never received them. Here is a short list of problems experienced in Election 2004:

POLLING PLACES. While it was heartening that apparently a record number of Americans came to the polls, it was discouraging that in many places, election officials seemed unprepared to handle the surge, despite the fact that record numbers had been predicted for weeks. Moreover, there were reports ranging from election officials randomly and inappropriately asking for identification from voters to the existence of a persistent rumor in some urban neighborhoods that voters with outstanding traffic tickets would be arrested.

PROVISIONAL BALLOTS. When voters are not on a registration list, they may request a provisional ballot, a fail-safe mechanism that was supposed to be a key reform in the Help America Vote Act (HAVA). But callers to Common Cause often expressed concern about what would happen to a vote cast on a provisional ballot.

ABSENTEE BALLOTS. Millions of Americans voted early and voted absentee this year. In news reports and in the calls we received at Common Cause before Election Day, voters, including disabled voters, senior citizens, and students, complained that they had not received their absentee ballots on time. Some were not allowed to vote because the voting list said they had already voted absentee, even if they had not.

VOTING MACHINES. Voting equipment remains a serious deficiency despite the promises made after the 2000 election debacle. A shortage of machines meant longer lines. There was no recount battle, but the lack of voter-verified paper trails on most electronic voting machines made credible recounts impossible.

What Needs to Be Done?

STRENGTHEN THE VOTING RIGHTS ACT. The next Congress will have no more important task than to extend the historic Voting Rights Act, which expires in 2007. This law is the bedrock of protection for minority voters and must be strengthened and extended. While the most egregious and obvious forms of discrimination were eliminated by this act, we continue to see insidious efforts to keep minorities from the polling place.

ADDRESS REGISTRATION PROBLEMS. Registration must no longer be a barrier to voting. Too often, lengthy pre-election deadlines and voter list mistakes disenfranchise voters. As a starting point, current laws must be followed in the spirit in which they were intended—to enable eligible voters to cast votes that are counted. Election Day registration should become a national standard.

ENFORCE LAWS AGAINST VOTER SUPPRESSION/INTIMIDATION. The U.S. Department of Justice and state and local authorities must have in place programs to protect Americans from efforts to intimidate.

They must make monitoring and defending the right to vote a top priority.

DEVELOP UNIFORM PROVISIONAL BALLOTS STANDARDS. Provisional ballots must be fully implemented as a meaningful safety net for voters when there are problems with registration or identification requirements. Every provisional ballot cast by an eligible voter should be counted.

FIX THE VOTING MACHINES. The nation still has not fixed the machinery of voting. Millions of Americans voted on discredited punch-card or lever machines. About one-third of voters used electronic voting machines that are unreliable and insecure. We must find the best technology for voting, and electronic voting machines need to supply voter-verified paper trails.

DEVELOP POLL-WORKER TRAINING AND RECRUITMENT PROGRAMS. Poll workers are the backbone of the nation's voting system. But too often poll workers fail to apply established laws and procedures, often because of a lack of training. Government and voters rights advocates must develop a new model for staffing polling places on Election Day.

FULLY IMPLEMENT THE VOTER DATABASE PROVISION OF HAVA. As most states face a 2006 Help America Vote Act (HAVA) deadline for establishing statewide voter databases, we must ensure that all registered voters are in fact on official voter lists and that the process of establishing the databases is open to the public.

INCREASE VOTER EDUCATION. Voters need more information about voting—easily accessible, widely distributed material on their rights as voters and the mechanics of voting. While voters have a responsibility to be informed, elections officials must do their part to inform them.

EXPAND ELECTION DAY. The turnout in the 2004 presidential election was encouraging and exciting. But the United States still has one of the lowest voter participation rates in the world. We should continue to knock down another barrier to voting—a lack of time—by expanding the ways in which and the time during which people can vote.

Don't Just Mobilize— Organize

Jane McAlevey is the executive director of Service Employees International Union Local 1107 in Las Vegas, Nevada.

JANE MCALEVEY

Don't mourn—*organize*! The classic union motto. So simple. We all agree with it, right? It is not something we need to seriously reflect on, right? We can just print it on a placard and stick it up on the wall by the coffee machine, right?

Wrong.

In fact, for the past few decades the progressive movement has worked under a different motto: Don't mourn—*mobilize*! And we have gotten good at mobilizing. In the 2004 presidential election, we set the movement record for mobilizing. And we lost.

Our emphasis on mobilizing is structured right into many of our leading organizations, from MoveOn to Greenpeace, temporary voter coalitions, and more. But experience has shown that organizations that are not built around organizing, per se, are ill-equipped for that task and will fail.

By "organizing," I mean an approach that has at its core a *day-to-day, direct relationship with the base*, and that uses this relationship to challenge people's core assumptions, to move them from individual to collective action, to teach workers and regular folks how to take on powerful foes and win on issues that matter.

There are simply no shortcuts to this. We know this because we have spent the past twenty years looking for one and have not found it. Right now, the fashionable shortcut is using the Internet. Ten years ago it was direct mail, robo phones, phone banks, opinion research, and "sophisticated media." None of this is bad; of course it is a good thing to poll and message and phone and communicate in better ways. All of this is important, and all of it adds up to more wins and a stronger movement. But none of this can replace organizing. It must be in addition to it.

In sorting out the election, the right's use of fear is emerging as a central theme. Unions deal with this every day—we are the antifear experts. Fear is a big factor in every organizing drive. Voting for a union and even fighting for it means overcoming fear of retaliation. This is basically loss of livelihood; this is not at all trivial.

The usual formulation is that fear leads people to vote against their own interests. So workers vote against unions, or Americans vote for a president who will lead them into disastrous wars and give away the treasury to the richest of the rich.

This formulation, however, is not helpful. If people really vote against their own interests, then there is no way out. But, in fact, people don't do that. The problem is not that people vote against their interests but that their expectations of what might be possible to win are so low that they define their interests in a distorted way. For example, if voting out the union is the only way to keep food on the table, then that is in your interest. If you think having good wages, health insurance, a pension, and a safe work environment are things you have no realistic chance of ever winning, then you don't risk the food on the table for them. Likewise, if you don't think the federal government might ever do anything good for you, you might settle for a president who promises "security."

The fear problem is, at root, a problem of low expectations. The key is to raise expectations—to get people to believe, through constant and direct experience, that they not only have the right to more, but that they can actually win more.

Taking the Initiative DAVID D. SCHMIDT

David D. Schmidt is director of the Initiative Resource Center in San Francisco and editor of the newsletter *Initiative & Referendum: The Power of the People!*

With Republicans controlling all three branches of the federal government, progressives will, in the near term at least, have to look to the initiative. But there isn't a moment to lose: in many states, measures must be finalized and petitioned (or approved by legislatures) in 2005 to be on the ballot in November 2006.

Initiatives to raise the minimum wage, fund clean energy development, and restrict the size of factory farms, proven winners in recent state elections, ought to be introduced where appropriate. Statewide ballot measures requiring voting machines to have verifiable paper trails would suffice until enough momentum is built in Congress for federal legislation.

With voters overwhelmingly supporting initiatives to raise the minimum wage in Nevada and Florida—both "red" states—it's conceivable to expect that minimum wage initiatives would pass almost anywhere.

Colorado voters passed an initiative requiring the state's electric utilities to develop clean, renewable energy sources. And voters in at least two heartland states have recently passed initiatives to restrict the growth of factory hog farms—a hot-button issue in the rural Midwest and Great Plains.

In twenty-four states and the District of Columbia, voters can put initiatives on state ballots by citizen petition and pass them by popular vote. In all states except Delaware, legislatures can put such propositions on the 2006 ballot as state constitutional or bond measures.

As long as Tom DeLay controls the House of Representatives,

Democrats' Congressional strategy will be primarily defensive. Progressives will need to match that with positive proposals on state ballots, something along the lines of the 1994 "Contract with America" that helped Republicans win a majority in the House for the first time in half a century.

Well-worded ballot initiatives can blaze a trail to a progressive victory in 2006. After all, who would publicly oppose an "Honest Vote Count," a "Living Wage," or a "Clean Energy/Clean Land" initiative? And in the twenty-four states, mostly in the West, where voters can put initiatives on the ballot by citizen petition and pass them by popular vote, there's nothing Tom DeLay or anybody else can do to stop them.

INDEPENDENT MEDIA

3

How to Work with Your Local Media HOLLY MINCH

Holly Minch is the director of the SPIN Project at the Independent Media Institute. She coedited, with Kim Haddow and Laura Saponara, the 2004 book *Loud and Clear in an Election Year.*

Republicans swept this election for three reasons:

••• They have learned to communicate under the level of policy. They're not just talking about programs and plans; they're also creating meaning with talk of right and wrong. The Values Thing = The Vision Thing.
••• They are not afraid to be simple. They are not afraid to make straightforward declarative statements that claim the debate and advance their worldview. They recognize that there is no time for equivocating in a news cycle that lasts about thirty seconds.
••• They are willing to do what works. They set priorities and pursue them with relentless focus.

November 2, 2004, was the culmination of thirty-five years of persistent organizing, smart communication strategy, and sheer force of will. It will take us time, too—but not that long, since more Americans are actually closely aligned with progressive, pro-democracy values.

So how do we win those Americans over?

We need to prioritize. We can't keep operating in single-issue silos. Instead we must line up those issues like dominoes so they all fall into place. And in that line, one domino will have to fall first. And other issues will have to wait in line while that happens.

The only mandate that came out of this election is this: Progressives must communicate their values more effectively to voters. We must talk about our goals in ways that people can hear. We must make meaning with our language in order to make our goals meaningful. That kind of communication will require deep listening, careful thought, and real respect for the voters we are trying to win.

As a progressive community, we need to avail ourselves of every possible opportunity to communicate our values and vision for a new America. Here are a few news-making opportunities we can use to advance the progressive agenda:

CIRCULATE COMMENTARIES AND EDITORIALS BROADLY. Use outlets like American Forum and the Progressive Media Project to place timely op-eds in outlets across the nation.

BE PREPARED. We don't know the dates, but we know we'll have to fight some high-intensity defensive battles soon. Prepare your talking points, craft your letters to the editor, and practice your radio call-in rap, because we'll need full-scale media efforts to galvanize public opinion on some major battles that are looming: saving Social Security, promoting immigration reform, blocking bad judicial nominations, and fending off attacks on *Roe v. Wade*.

CHECK EDITORIAL CALENDARS. These can help you tailor and time your media efforts to stories media outlets are already planning on covering. Here is a sample of issues to push on particular dates:

APRIL 15: TAX DAY. Corporate tax breaks, tax cuts for the wealthy.

APRIL 22: EARTH DAY. Local and national environmental issues.

MAY: FIFTY-FIRST ANNIVERSARY OF *BROWN V. BOARD OF EDUCATION*. Public education and race issues.

MAY 8: MOTHER'S DAY. Mothers of soldiers killed in Iraq, working mothers, day care.

JULY 4: INDEPENDENCE DAY. Independence from foreign oil with a call for clean energy.

LATE AUGUST: BACK TO SCHOOL. Public education.

SEPTEMBER 5: LABOR DAY. Struggles of working families, health care, minimum wage.

NOVEMBER 24: THANKSGIVING DAY. Genetically modified foods, social service groups.

Indy Media Outlets EVAN DERKACZ

AIR AMERICA RADIO. After a wobbly start, New York–based Air America Radio is starting to feel its oats as it expands to forty stations in markets from Columbus, Ohio, to Anchorage, Alaska. Though sometimes referred to as "the left's answer to Rush Limbaugh," don't be fooled. Despite the naked partisanship there is one important difference: the rants are fact based. You can also find the station's witty commentary and original newscasts via the Web or satellite radio.

PACIFICA RADIO. While the granddaddy of alternative broadcasting, Berkeley's Pacifica Radio, has only five official stations, dozens of affiliates air its programming nationwide. Pacifica's fifty-year commitment to being "listener sponsored" allows it to remain free of the demons that haunt the profit-driven mainstream media. In addition to original newscasts, Pacifica offers a host of politically charged shows, including, unsurprisingly, *Democracy Now!*

FREE SPEECH TV. Boulder, Colorado's Free Speech TV is for those who "hate TV." Broadcast on the DISH Network satellite television, this not-for-profit outfit airs independently produced documentaries and aims at "empowering global citizens by exposing abuse of power in all its forms and by highlighting efforts of resistance." Think Discovery Channel for progressives.

LINKTV. San Francisco's LinkTV believes there's absolutely nothing but the imagination that confines TV to local, or even national, perspectives. By offering programming that focuses on worldwide issues, LinkTV hopes to promote a global perspective and with it, an active participation in the world.

ALTERNET. And then, of course, there is your very own AlterNet (www.alternet.org). Check in each day—or two or three or more times a day—to read smart commentary, well-reported news sto-

ries, a smattering of the best progressive media, and the best of the
blogosphere.

Notable programs broadcast through various outlets:

- ••• Awarding-winning journalist Amy Goodman's
  Democracy Now!, the largest public media collaboration in the United States, is produced and broadcast
  from a firehouse in New York. Goodman's program
  harkens back to the golden age of hard-nosed,
  public-first journalism, putting Ted Koppel, Peter
  Jennings, and the Fox cheerleading squad to shame.
  Find *DN!* on satellite TV, radio, and the Internet.
- ••• Jon Stewart's *Daily Show*, a satirical look at current
  events, provides some of the smartest, most incisive
  commentary on TV.
- ••• The Fairness and Accuracy in Reporting (FAIR)
  radio show, *CounterSpin*, is a weekly roundup of "the
  news behind the headlines." It reaches 125 stations
  nationwide.
- ••• Radio talk-show host Ed Schultz is not your cookie-
  cutter liberal. He hunts, eats red meat, and is first to
  point out the failures of the Democratic Party. "I
  think I have the old traditional Democratic values,"
  says Schultz, age 50. "I think I represent the people
  who take their shower after work." Schultz's show,
  The Ed Shultz Show, is broadcast on seventy stations
  nationwide via the Democracy Radio Network.
- ••• Broadcast out of Boulder, Colorado, every week for
  nearly twenty years, David Barsamian's *Alternative
  Radio* highlights progressive guests and issues and
  offers a simple, intimate atmosphere for discussion.
- ••• *RadioNation*'s Marc Cooper has been bringing progressive news and commentary to the airwaves since
  1995. Cooper brings leading journalists, authors,
  and activists to seventy stations nationwide.

The Blogging MARKOS
Revolution MOULITSAS ZÚNIGA

Markos Moulitsas Zúniga founded DailyKos.com in 2002. It is now the largest political blog, averaging over 500,000 hits daily. Markos came to the United States as a child refugee from war-torn El Salvador and later served in the U.S. Army.

The words *open source* were once the domain of the techno-geeks—a counterculture movement driven by the radical notion that software development should be a collaborative process, with source code freely available to anyone for manipulation and improvement. The kicker? Any changes made to that software must be rereleased to the public. For free.

The software that powers the vast majority of Web servers doesn't come from Microsoft. It is called Apache, and it's open source. So is Linux, a complete operating system. The Macintosh operating system is based on open-source software. Firefox, easily the best browser available to Web surfers, is proof that open-source developers can develop user-friendly software. There are even open-source office suites (offering spreadsheet and word processing software) and open-source blogging tools (DailyKos.com runs on one).

It's not just the egalitarian ideal of free software at work here. Firefox is far more secure than Internet Explorer because hundreds of thousands of hackers worldwide can patch security holes in it within hours of discovering them. At Microsoft, such holes must wind their way through the Redmond office bureaucracy for weeks or longer before they get patched.

The key lesson here: more input is better.

Open-Source Journalism

In early February 2005, a handful of bloggers at DailyKos.com started to look at a White House correspondent named Jeff Gannon, who was employed by an organization called

Talon News. Gannon had come to their attention after media watchdog group Media Matters put a spotlight on softball questions he lobbed at White House spokesmen and President Bush himself.

Suddenly, hundreds of DailyKos readers and other bloggers, like those of Atrios and AMERICAblog, starting peeling away layer after layer of lies and deceit. "Jeff Gannon" was actually "Jim Guckert," and Talon News was merely a front organization for GOPUSA. And the situation got uglier. Guckert was found to own various domain names for military-themed gay escort services and was actually a male escort.

So we had a prostitute pretending to be a journalist, working for a Republican group pretending to be a news organization, who was given access to the White House and the president to lob softball questions at press conferences.

The revelations offered a good insight into the depths and reach of the White House propaganda machine, but the whole episode revealed something else: that hundreds of people had worked collectively to expose the various threads of the story. It was an achievement without precedent, carried out by the open-source investigative crew. Guckert may have been the first target, but he won't be the last.

Open-Source Activism

Street activism is old school. It wasn't too long ago that an industrial economy encouraged top-to-bottom hierarchies and prized those who followed orders. Activism followed that model, too, with a few leaders controlling the levers of street activism. If I wanted to start a boycott effort, I had little recourse other than to perhaps convince a Jesse Jackson type to join the effort. Anyone without connections, and without years of work within activist communities, was shut out of the process.

A few weeks before Election Day 2004, Sinclair Broadcast Group Inc., the owner of several dozen television stations, ordered its stations to preempt their programming to air an anti-Kerry documentary the day before the election. Establishment activists met this outrageous act by a corporation given use of the public's broadcast spectrum with hand wringing, but little action.

However, a couple of DailyKos readers rallied on the site, recruited the necessary talent, and created BoycottSinclair.com, a site dedicated to targeting and boycotting Sinclair's advertisers. Then hundreds of participants documented commercials airing on their local Sinclair stations, while others researched those advertisers, dug up their contact information, and published it. At that point, thousands of others called and wrote letters to those advertisers to express their displeasure. These actions helped tank Sinclair stock, and the pressure forced the company to scale back its plan and air a vastly abbreviated version of the controversial documentary.

The BoycottSinclair.com participants had no pedigree, nothing to give them "cred" as activists. But it didn't matter. Technology now allows those with the necessary skills and dedication to affect change in ways previously out of reach for the amateur activist.

Open-Source Politics

Political campaigns still prefer to work in that industrial mode—top to bottom, with worker bees following the orders of a small set of "strategists" calling all the shots. It's a model that has alienated people in our modern information age. Why would people schooled in the virtues of "self-initiative" and being "proactive" want to perform the electoral equivalent of screwing two bolts on Henry Ford's Model T assembly line? The idea of licking stamps and stuffing envelopes does not inspire many would-be activists who crave a real challenge and want to contribute to a greater cause.

Joe Trippi, looking for a way to maximize the limited resources of the insurgent Howard Dean presidential campaign, had the "idea that changed everything"—using the Web as a place to organize and, even better, allowing those Web-based supporters to take charge of their little bit of turf, whether it was organizing locally or providing solid advice that the campaign could then implement. It was chaotic, it was sometimes ugly, but it was about as open source a campaign as has ever been seen. And Dean's movement survived the cataclysm of his and Kerry's devastating losses. Once people had a taste of being valued contributors to a political campaign, they were not about to let go.

Unlike Dean, Kerry enjoys no lasting legacy from his presidential run. Kerry's was a traditional top-to-bottom campaign that gave supporters little to do beyond the standard political fare—licking envelopes, canvassing door to door, watching thirty-second spots, and voting. Meanwhile, the emotional connection Dean made with his supporters has landed him at the top of the Democratic National Committee.

Open-Source Limitations

While it would be nice to claim this new open-source movement as the purest manifestation of democracy in our politics, that's not necessarily the whole truth. The movement is heavily dependent on people who are online and excludes a great number of people—especially the poor and nonwhite—who don't have access to a computer. And because it also requires at least a basic comfort level with technology, it excludes the elderly and those with lower education levels.

Open-source politics isn't the be-all and end-all of politics or a replacement for traditional journalism, activism, and all aspects of a political campaign. It's merely another tool in our toolbox.

Yet it's a tool without limit. It's impossible to guess how it will evolve over the coming years, and what impact it will have on the political process. Open-source politics is not something that anyone can plan, not even those of us in the middle of this revolution. It is driven by the ideas, hard work, and initiative of thousands, potentially millions, of people turning their home computers into genuine political weapons.

The Top Ten Blogs

In January 2005, we at AlterNet asked our readers about their online reading habits, but mostly about what blogs they read and why. We were amazed that almost 8,000 readers responded to our survey. And the results are revealing.

For starters, two-thirds of our readers visit blogs. About 80 percent of those readers said they read "political" blogs, while 42 percent said they read "general interest" blogs. Not only do they read them, but a healthy 10 percent of our readers said they have their own blog.

Asked why they read blogs, more than half (56 percent) said they did so because they "keep me informed," while 40 percent said the blogs "go deeply into issues that I care about."

Then we got to the meat of it all: what are our readers' favorite blogs? DailyKos is the winner, in first place. Here is the top-ten list:

1. DailyKos (www.dailykos.com): "political analysis and other daily rants on the state of the nation" from Markos Moulitsas.
2. TomDispatch (www.tomdispatch.com): "a regular antidote to the mainstream media" from Tom Englehardt.
3. Talking Points Memo (www.talkingpointsmemo.com): from Joshua Micah Marshall.
4. Eschaton (www.atrios.blogspot.com): from Duncan Black, a 32-year-old "recovering economist."
5. Wonkette! (www.wonkette.com): a Washington DC–based blog that is a self-proclaimed "guide to DC politics and culture, sort of," from Ana Marie Cox.
6. The Daily Howler (www.dailyhowler.com): "a Socratic critique of the Washington press corps" from Bob Somerby, a former editorial writer at the *Baltimore Sun.*

7. Informed Comment (www.juancole.com): "thoughts on the Middle East, history, and religion" from Juan Cole, a history professor at the University of Michigan.

8. Liberal Oasis (www.liberaloasis.com): "where the Left is right and the Right is wrong."

9. MyDD (www.mydd.com): a political blog from Jerome Armstrong and Chris Bowers.

10. This Modern World (www.thismodernworld.com): first he did a syndicated cartoon, and now Tom Tomorrow has a popular blog.

DO-IT-YOURSELF
ORGANIZING
4 ————————————

How to Hold
a House Party

Rachel Neumann is the rights and liberties editor of AlterNet. She writes for *The Nation, Dissent,* and other publications.

You do not have to be a diva, a Stepford wife, or a social butterfly to hold a house party. You don't even have to be able to open a bottle of wine successfully. A house party is just an event, held in your home, to which you invite people you know as well as like-minded people you want to know better. It's a place to brainstorm strategies for change, as well as a chance to build a larger progressive community. Food, music, and drinks go a long way toward creating an environment that encourages creativity and inspiration.

Step 1: Create a Common Base of Knowledge

It's hard to start a project when everyone is coming to the table with different levels of knowledge of what is going on. Start by asking five to ten people you know to read this book (and/or some other book that has inspired you) and come to a house party at your home. If half of them show up, it's fine. And if a whole book feels like too much, find an essay or section that you feel was particularly inspiring and ask folks to read that. Or invite them over for a home movie screening—you can find films to watch at www.filmstoseebeforeyouvote.com.

Step 2: Create a Common **Vision**

One of the key aspects of leadership and change is vision. Everyone's a critic, as they say, but to create change requires a sense of where you want this country to go, not just what's wrong with it now. Ask everyone to write his or her vision for America on a piece of paper. Be as concrete here as possible. Read everyone's vision aloud and see whether there are common themes. Once you have come as close to a common vision as possible, you can begin to craft ways to move toward that vision.

Step 3: Assess Your Common Strengths **and Strategize**

A key to being effective organizers for change is to have a sense of what skills and resources you have so that you can plan your project based on your skills. Assess your strengths. Start by having your guests write down five things they like to do and are good at doing. Go through the ideas one by one and brainstorm how this interest or skill could be applied to making political change. For example, if a number of people put "reading" on their list, this interest could be applied to holding teach-ins, creating fact sheets, or getting together a progressive reading list for schools and libraries.

Step 4: Fix **a Goal**

Now that you have looked at your skills, return to the vision part. Keeping your skills in mind, now is the time to create some goals. Ask people to identify in their community some things they would most like to change: reform of commercial rent laws, changing school board members, or getting more accessible child care. It helps to start with a *goal* that is local and a *vision* that is national.

Step 5: Expand Your Network **Locally and Nationally**

How do you let others know what you are doing? What are other people doing? Networks and friends may be able to help with finances, expertise, media knowledge, or just

G
E
T
T
I
N
G

A
C
T
I
V
E

encouragement. Let people know about your vision first, before you focus on your specific project, goals, or what you would like help with. Your vision is your broadest recruiting tool. Pick a more public place for your next meeting and publicize it in the local newspaper or online community.

Shop Blue

DEANNA ZANDT

We all try to be aware of where we're spending our money, and often it's difficult (especially in rural areas) to get away from putting money into transnational corporations that don't have our best interests in mind. But as BuyBlue.org has shown, some corporations are certainly better than others.

Buy Blue has been tracking campaign donations from major industries, covering everything from retail shopping to entertainment to technology companies. The results are surprising in some cases (Costco is a big Democratic supporter) while others are beyond obvious (Wal-Mart gave over $2 million to Republicans).

The power of the almighty dollar has certainly become clear after the 2004 elections, and Buy Blue was started to provide information to consumers so that they could "vote with their wallets to support businesses that abide by sustainability, workers' rights, environmental standards, and corporate transparency."

The numbers from retail shopping alone are telling. Giving a majority of their political contributions to Republican campaigns and candidates were Wal-Mart, Circuit City, JC Penney, Sears, May Department Stores (which owns Filene's, Lord & Taylor, and Kaufman's, among others), Limited Brand (which owns Express, Limited, Victoria's Secret, and Bath & Body Works, among others), Saks, Home Depot, Target, and Amazon.com. Giving at least 93 percent of their contributions to Democratic candidates and campaigns were Price Club/Costco, Barnes & Noble, and Bed Bath & Beyond.

Who knew the Fruit of the Loom guys were red? They gave 100 percent of their contributions to Republicans, while other clothiers such as J. Crew, Calvin Klein, and Foot Locker placed their bets on the Democrats.

The award for "Best Toeing-the-Line" statement in campaign contributions is a tie between Anheuser-Busch, with 56 percent of its money going to Republicans, and Shell Oil, with 56 percent of its money going to Democrats.

In the technology arena, search engines drew the starkest comparisons: Yahoo! gave 99 percent ($99,000) of its total campaign contributions to Republicans, while Google put 100 percent of its $72,000 into Democratic campaigns. "Googling" something might take on a whole new meaning in the coming years.

BuyBlue.org is being expanded to eventually become a repository of information on each corporation listed, giving statistics on where the company stands on social issues and the ability for consumers to take action by sending letters of praise or complaint. Best of all, for each red company listed, Buy Blue offers several blue alternatives where you can spend your hard-earned dollars. Future plans include creating a Wiki of company information, where users contribute to and edit the ratings for each company listed . . . so keep your dollars peeled.

The Audacity of Hope BARACK OBAMA

On July 27, 2004, the "skinny kid with the funny name" stepped up to the podium at the Democratic National Convention and delivered a speech that electrified the cavernous room—and millions of living rooms across America. It was a speech that was at once intellectual and emotional, as well as progressive and patriotic. On November 2, 2004, Obama handily won the race for an Illinois seat in the U.S. Senate. The following is an excerpt from the convention speech, which we at AlterNet thought was an appropriate note to end a book about the future of progressive politics in America.

The greatness of our nation is not the height of our skyscrapers, or the power of our military, or the size of our economy. Our pride is based on a very simple premise, summed up in a declaration made over 200 years ago: "We hold these truths to be self-evident, that all men are created equal. That they are endowed by their Creator with certain inalienable rights. That among these are life, liberty, and the pursuit of happiness."

That is the true genius of America—a faith in simple dreams, an insistence on small miracles. That we can tuck in our children at night and know that they are fed and clothed and safe from harm. That we can say what we think, write what we think, without hearing a sudden knock on the door. That we can have an idea and start our own business without paying a bribe. That we can participate in the political process without fear of retribution, and that our votes will be counted—at least, most of the time.

We are called to reaffirm our values and our commitments, to hold them against a hard reality and see how we are measuring up to the legacy of our forebears, and the promise of future generations. And fellow Americans—Democrats, Republicans, Independents—I say to you: We have more work to do. More work to do for the workers I met in Galesburg, Illinois, who are losing their union jobs at the Maytag plant that's moving to Mexico and now are having to compete with their own children for jobs that pay seven bucks an hour. More to do for the father that I met who was losing his job and choking back the tears, wondering how he would pay $4,500 a month for the drugs his son needs without the health benefits that he counted on. More to do for the young woman in East Saint Louis, and thousands more like her, who has the grades, has the drive, has the will, but doesn't have the money to go to college.

Now don't get me wrong. The people I meet—in small towns and big cities, in diners and office parks—they don't expect government to solve all their problems. They know they have to work hard to get ahead—and they want to. Go into the collar counties around Chicago and people will tell you they don't want their tax money wasted—by a welfare agency or by the Pentagon. Go into any inner-city neighborhood and folks will tell you that government alone can't teach our kids to learn—they know that parents have to teach, that children can't achieve unless we raise their expectations and turn off the television sets and eradicate the slander that says a black youth with a book is acting white. They know those things.

People don't expect government to solve all their problems. But they sense, deep in their bones, that with just a slight change in priorities, we can make sure that every child in America has a decent shot at life, and that the doors of opportunity remain open to all. They know we can do better. And they want that choice.

And, in America, it's not enough for just some of us to prosper. For alongside our famous individualism, there's another ingredient in the American saga—a belief that we're all connected as one people. If there is a child on the south side of Chicago who can't read, that matters to me, even if it's not my child. If there's a senior citizen somewhere who can't pay for their prescription drugs and has to choose between medicine and the rent, that makes my life poorer, even if it's not my grandparent. If there's an Arab-American family being rounded up without benefit of an attorney or due process, that threatens my civil liberties. It is that fundamental belief, it is that fundamental belief—I am my brother's keeper, I am my sister's keeper—that makes this country work. It's what allows us to pursue our individual dreams and yet still come together as one American family. *E pluribus unum.* Out of many, one.

There is not a liberal America and a conservative America—there is the United States of America. There is not a Black America and a White America and Latino America and Asian America—there's the United States of America.

The pundits like to slice and dice our country into red states and blue states; red states for Republicans, blue states for Democrats. But I've got news for them. We worship an awesome God in the blue states, and we don't like federal agents poking around in our libraries in the red states. We coach Little League in the blue states, and yes, we've got some gay friends in the red states. There are patriots who opposed the war in Iraq and there are patriots who supported the war in Iraq.

We are one people, all of us pledging allegiance to the Stars and Stripes, all of us defending the United States of America. In the end, that's what this election is about. Do we participate in a politics of cynicism or do we participate in a politics of hope?

I'm not talking about blind optimism here—the almost willful ignorance that thinks unemployment will go away if we just don't think about it, or the health-care crisis will solve itself if we just ignore it. That's not what I'm talking about. I'm talking about something more substantial. It's the hope of slaves sitting around a fire singing freedom songs. The hope of immigrants setting out for distant shores. The hope of a young naval lieutenant bravely patrolling the Mekong Delta. The hope of a millworker's son who dares to defy the odds. The hope of a skinny kid with a funny name who believes that America has a place for him, too.

Hope in the face of difficulty. Hope in the face of uncertainty. The audacity of hope! In the end, that is God's greatest gift to us, the bedrock of this nation. A belief in things not seen. A belief that there are better days ahead.

I believe that we can give our middle class relief and provide working families with a road to opportunity. I believe we can provide jobs to the jobless, homes to the homeless, and reclaim young people in cities across America from violence and despair. I believe that we have a righteous wind at our backs and that as we stand on the crossroads of history, we can make the right choices and meet the challenges that face us.

America! If you feel the same energy that I do, if you feel the same urgency that I do, if you feel the same passion that I do, if you feel the same hopefulness that I do—if we do what we must do, then I have no doubt that all across the country, from Florida to Oregon, from Washington to Maine, the people will rise up . . . and this country will reclaim its promise, and out of this long political darkness a brighter day will come.

ACKNOWLEDGMENTS

Thanks to all the committed people who wrote for this book, sat for interviews, and contributed your work. The book would not exist without your generous support. Space constraints did not permit us to include all of your voices in the book, but we hope to publish many of these vital contributions on the book's Web site, StartMakingSense.org. We appreciate all you did during the struggle of 2004 and after to make our country a more humane place to live and work.

Special thanks to Mark Ritchie's efforts at National Voice (now the Center for Civic Participation) to distribute crucial information during the election and beyond.

Much appreciation is due to the Independent Media Institute/ AlterNet staff for overall support, especially Octavia Morgan, Holly Minch, Leigh Johnson, and Davina Baum. Thanks to Safir Ahmed for his wise overall editorial eye and Ginna Green for running down the permissions. On the logistical end, Deanna Zandt stayed up late hours wrangling the many sources of content from her NYC lair.

A big thank you to the IMI board as well, particularly board president Christine Triano and past president Larry Smith for their editorial smarts and years of steadfast support. We're also grateful for the wisdom of the other members of the board, including Denise Caruso, Sara Frankel, Kristen Grimm, Jeff von Kaenal, Robert Greenwald, Ludovic Blaine, and James Bernard.

Many thanks to AlterNet funders including The Nathan Cummings Foundation, The Arca Foundation, Wallace Global Fund, The Schumann Center for Media and Democracy, The McKay Foundation, Open Society Institute, The Glaser Progress Foundation, Working Assets, The Threshold Foundation, The Albert A. List Foundation, MoveOn.org, Bioneers, The TAUPO Fund, Branscomb Family Foundation, Axson and Bryan Morgan, Benno Friedman, Marlene Share, John Caulkins, our generous individual donors and the thousands of AlterNet readers who gave us your money and time.

Kudos to the Chelsea Green publishing team. Margo Baldwin is a great example of the daring and enterprising publishers who are helping to frame the future progressive agenda. We especially appreciate the efforts of John Barstow and Jennifer Nix to make this book happen.

From Lakshmi: Thanks to my mother, Shaili, and Beatrice for believing in me despite overwhelming evidence to the contrary; and, of course, a big shout out to Gauss for being Gauss.

From Don: Appreciation to my family, especially Mary Holman, who died just as this book was headed to the printer; special thanks to Vivian Dent, who made key parts of the book coherent; also appreciation to Robert Greenwald, Colin Greer, Rob McKay, Donna Edwards, Peter Teague, Jeffrey Chester, Ron Williams, Tai Moses, Harriet Barlow, Jane McAlevey, Jackie Wallace, Adam Hochschild, Helen Brunner, Wes Boyd, and Marty Feinberg for their invaluable support, encouragement, and acceptance.

ACKNOWLEDGMENTS

NOTES

NOTES

NOTES

NOTES

NOTES

CHELSEA GREEN PUBLISHING

the politics and practice of sustainable living

Shelter

Planet

Food

People